Changing Britain

Crown, parliament and people

Chris Husbands
Lecturer in History Education
University of East Anglia

CAMBRIDGE
UNIVERSITY PRESS

For Emily, Harriet and Victoria

Published by the Press Syndicate of the University of Cambridge
The Pitt Building, Trumpington Street, Cambridge CB2 1RP
40 West 20th Street, New York, NY 10011-4211, USA
10 Stamford Road, Oakleigh, Victoria 3166, Australia

First published 1992

Printed in Great Britain by Butler & Tanner Ltd, Frome

A catalogue record for this book is available from the British Library.

ISBN 0 521 40913 6 paperback

Designed and produced by Gecko Limited, Bicester, Oxon.
Picture research by Callie Kendall

Notice to teachers
Many of the sources used in this textbook have been adapted or abridged from the original.

Cover illustration: 'Whitehall, January 30th, 1649', reproduced by permission of Forbes Magazine Collection, Bridgeman Art Library

Acknowledgements
The author and publisher would like to thank the following for permission to use the illustrations on the following pages:

5, reproduced by courtesy of the Trustees of the British Library; 6, 10 (details of: Henry VII, James I, Charles I), 11 (details of: Edward VI, Mary I, Lady Jane Grey), 17, 19, 23, 28, 35, 38, 42 (details of: Charles I, Queen Anne), 43 (details of: James I, the 'Old Pretender', George I, George II), 86, National Portrait Gallery, London; 7, 69 (top), 81, Mary Evans Picture Library; 8 (bottom), on loan to Scottish National Portrait Gallery; 9, Aerofilms; 11 (Henry VIII), Board of Trustees of the Royal Armouries; 11 (detail of: Elizabeth I), The Master and Fellows of Trinity College, Cambridge; 13, Private Collection; 14, from John Derrick's *Image of Ireland,* 1581; by permission of the Syndics of the University of Cambridge Library; 15, Windsor Castle Royal Library. © 1992. Her Majesty The Queen; 30, 42 (William & Mary), 51, 90 (top), 92 (left), Mansell Collection; 32–33 (bottom), Hulton-Deutsch Collection; 36, by courtesy of the Board of Trustees of the Victoria & Albert Museum; 37, reproduced by courtesy of Trustees of the British Museum; 42 Charles II in Garter Robes by Sir Peter Lely, from the Duke of Grafton's private collection at Euston Hall in Suffolk; 43 (James II), 83 (bottom), The Master and Fellows of Magdalene College, Cambridge; 45 Private Collection/Bridgeman Art Library; 46 (Oliver Cromwell),The Master and Fellows of Sidney Sussex College, Cambridge; 48, © Sutherland Collection, Ashmolean Museum, Oxford; 51, by permission of the British Library/Bridgeman Art Library; 52 (top), Cambridge University Collection: copyright reserved; 52 (bottom), © Jeremy Nicholl, Impact Photos; 53 Associated Sports Photography; 56–57, 92–93, *Dixton Manor House,* Gloucestershire,by an unknown artist, c.1735, Cheltenham Art Gallery and Museums/Bridgeman Art Library; 62 (stocks at Stanton Harcourt), © K.R. Sporne 1988; 63, Tate Gallery, London; 66, reproduced by permission of the Marquess of Bath, Longleat House, Warminster, Wiltshire, Great Britain; 66–67, Dr Roger Schofield, Cambridge Group for the History of Population and Social Structure, Cambridge; 74 and 75 Prado, Madrid/Bridgeman Art Library; 78, Ian Hepburn; 83 (top left), Istituto e Museo di Storia della Scienza di Firenze, photo by Franca Principe; 84, National Trust, Petworth House, Sussex/Bridgeman Art Library; 87 Bibliotheek der Rijksuniversiteit te Utrecht; 89 Museum of London; 90 (bottom left), Thomas-Photos Oxford; 90 (bottom right), A.F. Kersting; 91, Guildhall Library; 92 (top), Topham Picture Source; 93 (left), Robert Harding Picture Library; 93 (bottom inset), A.J.H. & J.C. Sale.

Contents

Introduction

Britain in 1500

What was Britain like in 1500?

What would a visitor to Britain have noticed in 1500? What would he or she have thought about the people and their way of life? We can find out by looking at what one visitor wrote home.

Andreas Franciscus was an Italian who visited Britain in 1497. His ship landed at Dover, and he travelled on horseback across much of the country. He spent a lot of time exploring London. He did not actually visit Scotland, Wales, or Ireland. But he did write down the things he heard about these parts of Britain. It was his only visit to Britain and he wrote a long letter home to describe what he found.

As you use this book you will find out more about the land that Andreas visited, and the way it changed between 1500 and 1750.

Source A

This is an extract from Andreas's letter.

> The people are handsome and well-built. They are great lovers of themselves, and think they do anything better than other countries. They all wear very fine clothes and are very polite. The common people work hard at trade or at fishing, but the farmers are lazy. They keep an enormous number of sheep which give them best-quality wool. They eat very often, and sometimes more than is good for them, and even the common people are known to eat swans, rabbits, deer and sea birds.
>
> London is the capital. It stands on the banks of the river Thames and there is a beautiful bridge over the river. Nowhere have I seen a finer or more richly built bridge. London has every luxury you can imagine. There are workshops of craftsmen all over the town, which makes it very rich. But the streets of London are so badly paved that there is a huge amount of evil-smelling mud which lasts nearly all year round. In fact the whole country seems to have the same trouble with mud. Londoners have very fierce tempers and bad manners. London is the home of their king, who is very powerful.
>
> At the head of Scotland is a king who rules very fierce and brave tribes, who are always the enemies of the English and often at war with them.
>
> As regards Ireland, which is not far from Britain on the western side, I could say a few things, such as their life is poor and the men's clothing is made from rough greasy cloths and other things like this. But I would be wrong to put in writing things I had not seen myself, so I will leave it to people who can travel farther.

Andreas Franciscus, 1497

Source B   *London in about 1500. It is possible that this picture was given to King Henry VII. It shows the Tower of London with London Bridge in the background.*

● *How has the artist tried to make London look like a busy place?*

---

1 What does Andreas Franciscus tell us about:
◆ what people ate and wore
◆ London
◆ Londoners
◆ the English king
◆ Scotland
◆ Ireland?

2 a Which of the things that Andreas Franciscus tells us do you think we can rely on?
b Which of the things that Andreas Franciscus tells us do you think we cannot rely on?
c Are there any ways in which Andreas Franciscus agrees with the artist who painted Source B?

3 What other questions would you like to be able to ask Andreas about Britain in 1500?

1
A divided Britain?

How can we find out about Britain between 1500 and 1750?
What ideas do we get from different types of evidence?
In what ways was Britain divided?

▲ Source B *'The rich man and the poor man'. An engraving, 1569, by an unknown artist.*

● What are the main differences between the two people in the picture?
● Do Sources A and B show that Britain was divided? In what way?

Britain was divided in many more ways than the one you have just looked at. This book is about divisions in Britain, and about the problems they caused. It is also about the changes which took place between 1500 and 1750 – and about the ways in which some of those changes still affect our lives today.

◢ Source A *A banquet in the house of a sixteenth-century gentleman. Sir Henry Unton sits at the centre of the table and his wife, Lady Dorothy, sits on the right. The feasting is over, and the guests are watching a special show. Can you see the dancers, with their masks and torches?*

This picture is part of a much larger painting, completed in about 1596. It was ordered by Sir Henry's widow, on his death, and shows different scenes from his life.

● *What signs are there that Sir Henry Unton was a rich gentleman?*

7

Source C

Put to death! Catholic monks being killed for their beliefs in the 1530s, during the reign of Henry VIII. This picture comes from a Catholic book printed in 1587, at a time when Queen Elizabeth I had renewed such executions

Source D

On 30 January 1649, King Charles I was executed in Whitehall, London, in front of an enormous crowd of people. This painting is by an unknown Dutch artist. It was probably painted shortly after the execution.

Source E *The town of Berwick-upon-Tweed, on the border between England and Scotland. The defences were reinforced by Queen Elizabeth I in the 1580s. There used to be a strong castle, an 80-foot wide ditch and watch towers. The ramparts can still be seen. The old town was enclosed within fortified walls.*

1 Look at Sources C–E. How do they show that Britain was a divided land at this time?

2 Copy the table below, then fill in the second column to show how the sources in this unit help us to understand each statement.

	Source
◆ In 1500, Britain was made up of four separate nations: England, Wales, Scotland and Ireland. Gradually England increased its control over the rest of the British Isles.	
◆ In 1527, King Henry VIII argued with the Pope, and this led to arguments over religion and many changes in the Church. Some people were hanged or burnt for their religious beliefs.	
◆ Between 1642 and 1651 there was a civil war between King Charles I and Parliament, which involved all parts of Britain. In 1649, Charles I was executed. Fighting between the King's supporters and Parliament's army continued for many years.	
◆ Many people in Britain were very poor, and the number of poor people grew between 1500 and 1750. The government tried to stop poor people from begging by introducing harsh punishments.	

The power of

HENRY VII
(1485 –1509)

Henry Tudor was a Welsh noble-man who became the King of England and Wales in 1485 when he won the Battle of Bosworth. This battle brought to an end thirty years of civil war (the 'Wars of the Roses'). When he died, his son, Henry VIII, took over.

This is the 'family tree' of the kings and queens who ruled between 1485 and 1649. The dates given here show the length of each monarch's reign

Arthur
(died 1502)

Margaret   =   **James IV**
(died 1541)   **King of Scots**

James V
King of Scots
(died 1542)

Mary
Queen of Scots
(executed 1587)

JAMES I
(1603 – 25; James VI of Scots 1567–1625)   =   **Anne of Denmark**
James was King of Scotland before he became King of England too. Arguments over money, power and religion grew more bitter during his reign. When he died in 1625, his son, Charles, became king.

CHARLES I
(1625 – 49; executed)   =   **Henrietta Maria**
Charles argued with Parliament. In 1642, a civil war broke out between them. Charles lost the war, and he was executed in 1649. He is the only British king to have been put on trial and executed by his people.

the Monarchy

HENRY VIII = **six wives**
(1509 – 47)

Henry VIII was a strong king. He argued with the Pope about divorcing his wife. He made himself Head of the Church of England. His changes in the Church began a century of argument between Catholics and Protestants about religion.

Charles Brandon = **Mary**
Duke of Suffolk **(died 1533)**

Henry Grey = **Frances**
Duke of Suffolk **(died 1559)**

EDWARD VI
(1547– 53)

Edward was only a boy of 11 when his father Henry VIII died. Edward and his advisers were Protestants. The young king was controlled by rich, powerful nobles. During his short reign – Edward died at the age of 16 – new Protestant ideas began to take over.

MARY I
(1553 – 58)

Mary tried to restore the Catholic Church to power, but she died after only five years on the throne. She married King Philip of Spain, but died childless, so her half-sister Elizabeth became Queen.

ELIZABETH I
(1558 –1603)

Unlike her half-sister, Elizabeth was a Protestant. She became one of the most powerful and popular of the Tudors, especially after 1588 when the Spanish Armada, a fleet that tried to invade England, was defeated. She never married. When she died in 1603 she left no children. Her cousin James then took over.

JANE GREY
(9 –15 July 1553; executed 1554)

When Edward VI died, there was a struggle for power. He had named Lady Jane Grey as the next monarch. But after she had ruled for only nine days, she was overthrown. Mary replaced her as Queen. Jane Grey was executed.

2

What problems did the Tudors and Stuarts face?

In 1485, Henry Tudor defeated Richard III at the Battle of Bosworth. He became the new King of England. Over 150 years later, in 1649, King Charles I was executed.

How was England ruled between 1485 and 1649? What problems did kings and queens in the sixteenth century face?

Think about how Britain is ruled today. Who is the most powerful person in the country?

Today every adult can vote in elections to choose a government. The government makes decisions that affect us all. The Queen has very little influence over these decisions. In 1485, things were very different. England and Scotland each had a king or queen who ran the country. In Ireland there was no king. There, warlike chieftains controlled small areas of the country and fought each other.

How did the King rule?

When Henry VII became King of England in 1485, the court was the centre of government. It was made up of rich nobles, bishops, entertainers and servants. Although he asked other people for advice, the King made all the important decisions.

Source A

This is taken from an Act of Parliament passed during Henry VIII's reign.

'In many old histories and record books, it is clearly declared that this country of England is an empire…ruled by one supreme head, the King.'

Act of Appeals, 1533

Problem 1: Money

Where the monarch's money came from:

* **Land** – rents from land owned by the Crown, about one-quarter of all land in England

* **Customs duties** (e.g. on wool) – England traded with many countries

* **Taxes** raised by Parliament – they always agreed to taxes suggested by the King

* **Borrowing** – there were money lenders all over Europe

Henry VII realised that a poor king was weak. He began to try to build up the royal income (money). But the kings and queens who came after him were often short of money.

Source B   *A procession of Queen Elizabeth I in
about 1600. She is surrounded by the nobles and ladies of
her court.*
● *How has the artist made Elizabeth look the most
important person?*

Problem 2: Parliament

If the King wanted to turn to a larger group than his
closest advisers for help, he called together a
Parliament. Members of Parliament only met when
the King asked them, so they did not meet very often
or for very long.

Even so, Parliaments were still important. They
were the only occasions when the King met a fairly
large number of his people. There was a tradition that
no tax could be brought in unless Parliament agreed.
As time went on, rulers had more and more problems
persuading Parliament to give them money. When
Charles I could not get new taxes from Parliament,
he tried to do without the Parliament. This made
many people angry.

Source C

In this source, Henry VIII seems to suggest that
Parliament was very important. He was speak-
ing to Parliament when he said:

'I am at my most royal and powerful when I
meet together with Parliament.'

Henry VIII, 1536

Problem 3: Rebellions

The kings and queens of England also controlled
Wales and parts of Ireland. But there were many
rebellions against English rule.

They wanted to control Scotland too. There had
been fighting between England and Scotland for
many centuries and in 1513, there was another war
between the two countries. The Scottish were heavily
defeated at the Battle of Flodden, and the King of
Scotland, James IV, was killed. Later, the English
Queen Elizabeth I held the young Scottish Queen,
Mary, in prison for many years before executing her.
Eventually, in 1603, James VI of Scotland became
the King of England (James I), but there were still
disagreements between the two countries.

13

In 1567, the Irish chieftains surrendered to an English army, but for many years to come there were rebellions against English governors in Ireland.

The Tudors had many enemies in England, and there were many rebellions against them. There was no other way that the people could express their anger against the government.

Rebellion!

1495 An Irish rebellion was organised to try to overthrow Henry VII.

1497 Western Rising: a rebellion in Devon and Cornwall against Henry VII.

1536 The Pilgrimage of Grace: over 10,000 people from all over the North of England joined a rebellion to protest against religious changes.

1549 The year of two rebellions: one in Devon, and one in Norfolk and Suffolk, against Edward VI's government.

1554 Wyatt's Rebellion: 5,000 people from Kent marched on London to try to overthrow Mary.

1569 The Rebellion of the Northern Earls: noblemen in the North of England organised a rebellion against Elizabeth I.

1 Look back at pages 10–11. How did Henry VII become king? How did Henry VIII become king?

2 Most of the portraits on pages 10–11 were painted to make the person look impressive.
a How have the artists made the monarchs look important?
b Do you think they give a reliable idea of what the person really looked like?
c How are these portraits useful to us?

3 a Copy the following table, and fill it in.

Source	What it tells about the monarch's power	Reasons why it might/might not be reliable evidence
A B C D		

b Much of the evidence that you have looked at in this unit is unreliable. How can a historian use evidence that is not reliable?

4 Using the 'family tree' on pages 10–11, explain why there were problems about who should rule England in:
◆ 1547
◆ 1558
◆ 1603.

3

The rise of Parliament

Between 1500 and 1650 the kings and queens argued more and more with Parliament. Ideas about how the country should be ruled changed. Some people began to think Parliament should play a bigger part in running the country.

Why did this change take place?

Source A *Henry VIII opening Parliament in 1519. Henry is on the throne, with the members of his council, and the archbishops, near him. The noblemen are sitting in rows, and at the bottom of the picture the Commoners have squeezed in to hear the King.*

● *How does this picture suggest that the King made the important decisions?*

Who had most power?

Parliament only met when the King or Queen asked it to. The monarch could dismiss Parliament whenever he or she wanted. Source A gives you a good idea about who had most power in 1500. But after 1540 there was some new thinking about Parliament. Source B is an example of this new thinking.

Source B

'The highest and most absolute power in the kingdom of England is Parliament. If Parliament agrees to something, then we believe every man has agreed to it.'

Sir Thomas Smith, 1565

If Smith was right, Parliament was becoming more important in the sixteenth century. How can we explain this?

There are different explanations. Perhaps Parliament was being asked to do new things. Perhaps Parliament itself was changing. Look at the information about Parliament on the next page. For each development, work out how it made Parliament more powerful.

15

A Until 1500, the House of Lords was more important than the House of Commons. After 1500, merchants and traders, who sat in the Commons, became richer. So they felt that the House of Commons should become more important.

B Members of Parliament (MPs) began to think they had some special rights. Queen Elizabeth I told MPs that they could express their own opinions. Some MPs thought this meant they could discuss whatever they wanted. But Elizabeth I put one MP in prison because he kept trying to discuss things she did not like.

C Between 1585 and 1601, England was at war with Spain. It was a costly war. Members of Parliament supported the war and voted for taxes to pay for it. They thought this meant they should be able to make some decisions about the war.

D Between 1529 and 1536, Henry VIII made some very big changes in the way the Church was run. This was because he argued with the Pope, and set up his own Church of England. Henry wanted people to support him, so he asked Parliament to vote for his changes. The Members of Parliament whom Henry called together in 1529 met on and off for seven years. No Parliament before had met for so long. Parliament began to think of itself as the King's partner.

E Kings were often short of money. By 1500 the King needed Parliament to vote taxes to pay for fighting wars. Prices were rising quickly and the Crown's money problems got worse.

£430,000

£370,000

£140,000   £130,000

Income	Spending	Income	Spending
1500		1600	

---

1 Why did the King need Parliament?

2 Look at the different causes which led to Parliament becoming more important. Explain how the following factors made Parliament more powerful:
◆ money
◆ war
◆ religion.

3 Which of the causes do you think was most important? Arrange the causes A–E in order from most important to least important. Explain why you chose this order.

4 Use the ideas in this unit to design a large diagram showing why Parliament became more important.

4

James I and the Divine Right of Kings

Arguments between the Crown and Parliament became more and more bitter. In 1642 civil war broke out between King Charles I and Parliament. Some historians believe that the causes of this war were to do with the way in which James I and his son, Charles I, behaved. Others think James and Charles faced an impossible situation.

Did James I help to cause the Civil War?

A new king: James Stuart

Elizabeth I had no children. When she died in 1603, the English Crown passed to her cousin, James Stuart. James had been King of Scotland since he was a baby. He now became the first person to rule both countries. He became James I of England as well as James VI of Scotland.

Source A
James I of England, and James VI of Scotland. At the time of this painting he was about 55 years old.

Source B
This is a description of James written by a Frenchman who visited him in Scotland in 1584.

'James understands clearly and judges wisely. He is well-taught in languages, sciences and government. In short he is remarkably intelligent and has a high opinion of himself. But his manners are crude and he is lazy, letting others do all the work.'

M. de Fontenay, 1584

Source C
This description of James is rather different. The author fell out with James and wrote this fifteen years after the king died.

'He was fat. His tongue was too large for his mouth. He never washed his hands. He was crafty and cunning in small things but a fool in important matters. He left things to others to do.'

Sir Anthony Weldon, 1641

The 'Divine Right of Kings'

James believed in the 'Divine Right of Kings'. He believed that kings were appointed by God to defend the Church and the people. He expected people to obey him. Anyone who disobeyed the King was disobeying God.

The 'Divine Right of Kings': many people believed that the King's authority came from God.

● *Why do you think Parliament did not like these ideas?*

Source D

This is taken from a speech to Parliament made by James.

'Monarchy is the greatest thing on earth. Kings are rightly called gods since just like God they have power of life and death over all their subjects in all things. They are accountable to God only … so it is a crime for anyone to argue about what a king can do.'

James I, 1614

Problems for the King

James was forced to call the English Parliament because of his dreadful money problems. He had been left a huge debt by Elizabeth, but, unlike her, he had a family to look after. James did not like Parliament. He thought that MPs argued too much. He would have preferred them to do just as he told them.

Source E

This extract is from a letter written by James to the Spanish ambassador.

'The House of Commons is like a body without a head. The members give their opinions noisily. At their meetings nothing is heard except cries and shouts. I am surprised English kings ever allowed such a place to exist.'

James I, 1621

1 How did James I become king in 1603?

2 Look at Sources A, B and C.
a Write down two things that you can find out about James from each source.
b Write down any things which you can find out about James which are in more than one source.
c Which of these sources do you think is the most useful to a historian who wanted to find out about:

◆ what James looked like
◆ how good a king he was
◆ what people thought of him?

3 How did each of these things contribute to James's problems:

◆ his Scottish background
◆ his belief in the 'Divine Right of Kings'
◆ money
◆ Parliament?

5

Charles I: ruling without Parliament

Charles I became King in 1625. He shared his father's ideas about the Divine Right of Kings. Soon he was arguing with Parliament. They argued so much that between 1629 and 1640 Charles I decided to try to rule without Parliament. Some people called this period of eleven years the 'eleven years' tyranny'.

Was Charles I to blame for his argument with Parliament?

Source A *This portrait of Charles I on his horse was painted by an unknown artist.*

● *How would you describe the expression on the King's face?*

The arguments that James I had with Parliament about money and religion did not end in 1625. In 1629 Parliament told Charles that they would not give him money unless he agreed to a document called the 'Petition of Right'. This said that no taxes could be raised without Parliament's permission. Charles refused. He sent MPs away and decided to try to rule without Parliament. He would try to manage without the taxes which only Parliament could raise.

Instead, he now relied on two close advisers: William Laud and Thomas Wentworth, Earl of Strafford. And he looked for new ways to make money.

Changes in the Church

William Laud was Archbishop of Canterbury. He disliked Puritans (strong Protestants who wanted to 'purify' the Church). He wanted to make church services more elaborate. When he brought back stained-glass windows and more ceremony, Puritans thought he was trying to make England Catholic again.

Source B

'Nothing can be correct without some ceremonies, and in religion the more old-fashioned they are the better.'

William Laud, 1637

Source C

This is how Parliament accused Laud after the 1630s.

'Like a traitor he has tried to ruin true religion and replaced it with Catholic ideas. He has brought in Catholic ceremonies without any agreement and he has cruelly persecuted those who have opposed him.'

Impeachment Articles, 1641

Who should pay Ship Money?

Charles set out to find new ways of raising money. He borrowed a lot, and he also began to sell people the exclusive right to make things such as soap. These monopolies made those merchants who could no longer make the goods, very angry.

But the biggest argument was over Ship Money. This was originally a tax paid by people living on the coast to pay for a navy in wartime. In 1634 Charles asked for Ship Money even though there was no war. In 1635 he asked everyone in England to pay, not just people living by the coast. John Hampden, a rich landowner, refused to pay. In court, the judges agreed with Charles that Ship Money was legal.

Source D

This is taken from the speech made in court by John Hampden's lawyer.

'The king should take nothing from his subjects except with the agreement of Parliament.'

Court records, 1637

Source E

And this is taken from the verdict of the judges.

'The king should have the right to demand, and the people must pay, money for the defence of the kingdom.'

Sir Robert Berkely, Justice of the King's Bench, 1637

Crisis in Scotland

Religious arguments and Ship Money made Charles very unpopular. Until 1638 he coped. Then he made a big mistake. He argued with the Scots. Charles and Laud decided to try to force Scottish Protestants to use the English prayerbook. Most Scots were strong Protestants (called Presbyterians). The Scots refused and then rebelled. They formed an army. In 1640 they marched into England, and made demands on the King.

Source G

This is from the Covenant, or promise, made by Scottish people in 1638.

'We promise and declare that we shall with all our means and our lives defend our true Protestant religion, our freedoms and the laws of our kingdom. We will oppose all the new errors and corruptions.'

Scottish Covenant, 1639

Source H

The following is part of a letter from King Charles to his general in Scotland.

'Say what you need to these rebels. Your aim now must be to win time so that the crowds cause no damage until I can attack them. I will die rather than yield to these impertinent and awful demands.'

Charles I, 1639

Source F *When Laud tried to make the Scots use the English prayerbook, there were riots. This illustration, by a modern artist, is based on an engraving showing a riot in St Giles' Kirk, Edinburgh, in 1637.*

1 Which of the sources in this unit tell us about:
a opposition to Charles
b Charles's and Laud's attitudes to religion
c Charles's ideas about what a king could do
d Charles's character?

2 Work in groups. Using all the evidence in the sources in this unit, write an account of the problems that are to do with money, the Scottish issue, and religion, *either* from Charles I's point of view *or* from his opponents' point of view.

6

Civil war!

In April 1640 Charles was in a desperate situation. He had to call a Parliament to try to raise money to fight the Scots. Within two years he was at war with Parliament.

What went wrong? Why did civil war start?

The Short Parliament: 1640

Charles urgently needed money to pay for an army to crush the Scottish rebellion. The Scots were occupying Northumberland and threatened to come further south. He had to call Parliament. But MPs said that Charles had to deal with their complaints before they would vote him any money. Charles lost patience and after only three weeks he sent the MPs away.

Then disaster struck Charles. His army was beaten by the Scots, and Charles was forced to promise to pay money to the victorious army. The Crown was nearly bankrupt. In September Charles had to call another Parliament in order to raise some money.

The Long Parliament: 1640–60

When the new Parliament met, more than 400 out of 500 MPs agreed on what to do. They wanted to punish Charles's advisers, to change the Church, and to make sure Charles could not rule without Parliament again. They started by arresting Charles's close advisers, Laud and Strafford. Strafford was brought before MPs. Instead of being put on trial, a law was introduced which simply declared that he was guilty of treason. A huge crowd gathered outside Parliament and forced the House of Lords to pass the law. Strafford was then executed.

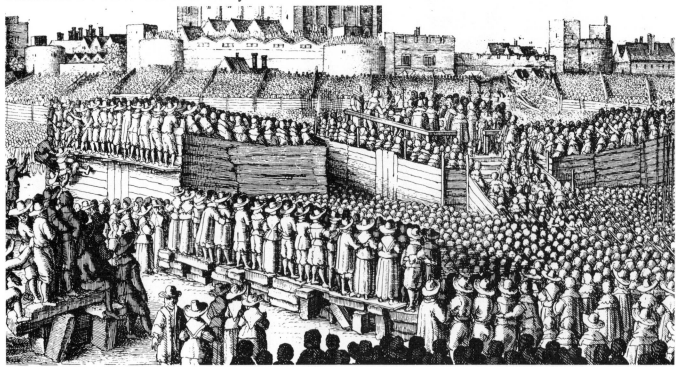

Source A *The execution of the Earl of Strafford on Tower Hill in London 1641. The artist suggests that a huge crowd came to see it.*

● *Why do you think so many people came?*

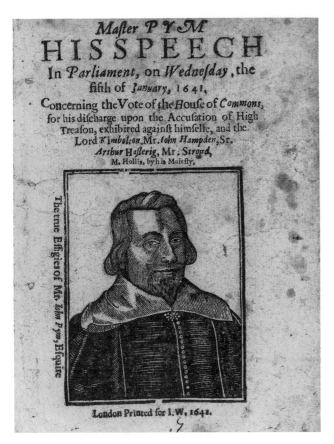

Master PYM

HIS SPEECH

In *Parliament*, on *Wednesday*, the fifth of *January*, 1641.

Concerning the Vote of the House of *Commons*, for his discharge upon the Accusation of High Treason, exhibited against himselfe, and the Lord *Kimbolton*, Mr. *Iohn Hampden*, Sr. *Arthur Haslerig*, Mr. *Strowd*, M. Hollis, by his Majesty,

The true Effigies of Mr. *Iohn Pym*, Esquire

London Printed for I.W. 1641.

Source B *Parliament's leader was John Pym. He believed that Charles could not be trusted. He was nicknamed 'King Pym'.*

● *Why do you think that was?*

Laws passed 1640 – 41 by the Long Parliament

✴ Ship Money abolished

✴ Monopolies abolished

✴ Selling knighthoods made illegal

✴ Parliament to choose the King's ministers

✴ Parliament to be called at least every three years

✴ Parliament could not be ended unless MPs agreed

Source C

This extract gives Charles's view of what Parliament was doing.

'All the troubles are caused by a handful of evil and ambitious people who want to change the government and Church and to put everyone under their own lawless power.'

Charles I, 1641

Source D

This source gives Parliament's view of what was going on.

'We will not allow a few people around the King, or even the King himself on his own, to decide what the law will be, especially as the King has always relied on a few individuals to help him.'

Grand Remonstrance, 1641

Rebellion in Ireland

In September 1641, the arguments between Charles and Parliament were interrupted by a Catholic rebellion in Ireland. An army was needed to put it down. But who would control it? In the past, the King had always controlled the army. But now Parliament did not trust the King. When MPs asked to be allowed to share command of the army, Charles believed they wanted to take all his power.

The war starts

Most of the laws passed by the Long Parliament were agreed by all MPs. Charles had no choice but to accept them. Some MPs thought these laws would now end the arguments, and they started to side with the King. But Pym and most of the others still did not trust him. Charles made a last attempt to take control. He arrived in the House of Commons with his soldiers to arrest five leading MPs. Unluckily for him, they had been tipped off and had slipped out.

Source E

Charles I's words were reported by an eye-witness.

> 'Well, I see all the birds have flown. I expect you to send them to me as soon as they return. If not, I will seek them myself, for their treason is foul.'

Charles I, 1642

Nottingham

This botched arrest was disastrous for Charles. It proved that the King could not be trusted. Parliament started to pass laws which the King had not agreed. Charles now decided Parliament had gone too far and left London to look for support. In August he raised an army. Parliament raised an army too. War had begun.

Source F

In August, Charles raised his flag in Nottingham. This was a signal that he was going to fight.

● *In this cartoon, what is the King's flag decorated with?*

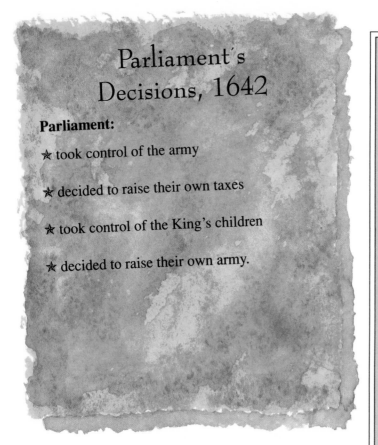

Parliament's Decisions, 1642

Parliament:

★ took control of the army

★ decided to raise their own taxes

★ took control of the King's children

★ decided to raise their own army.

---

1 Why did Charles I have to call Parliament in 1640?

2 Draw a timeline like this (although you will probably need to make your line much longer):

April   August
1640   1641   1642

a In *red*, mark and underline things that Members of Parliament did which made things worse between themselves and the King.

b In *blue*, mark and underline things that Charles did which made things worse between himself and the MPs.

c In *green*, mark and underline other things that made things worse between MPs and the King.

3 Why do you think MPs would not help Charles arrest the five Members?

4 Who do you blame for the start of the war? Explain your answer.

7
Taking sides

The Civil War lasted for nine years. As we have seen, it was an argument about several things: power, religion and money.

How did people decide whether to support the King or Parliament?

A divided country: how did people choose sides?

Civil wars are wars between people living in the same country. They can be very bitter. Friends might find themselves on different sides. Even people in the same family might fight each other. In 1642 people had to make up their minds: did they support the King or Parliament? Those who supported the King were called Royalists. Those who opposed the King were called Parliamentarians.

Source A

'You would think it strange if I should tell you there was a time in England when brothers killed brothers, cousins cousins and friends their friends.'

Letter from Sir John Oglander to his grandchildren, 1660s

- Can you think of any other examples of civil wars?

A divided country: did people *want* a war?

To answer this question, historians have looked at letters which were written during the 1640s. Read Sources B–E carefully.

Source B

This was written by one of the King's supporters.

'These are strange things for this country that has lived so long peacefully. It is, I say, a thing most horrible that we should fight a war with one another.'

Sir Henry Slingsby, 1640

Source C

Sir William Waller became one of Parliament's most famous generals. This letter was written to Sir Ralph Hopton, an old friend, who also became a famous general – for the King. In 1643 these two men commanded armies that fought against each other.

'The experience I have had of your worth and the happiness I have had from your friendship are wounding thoughts when I look at the present difference between us. My friendship with you is unchanged. But I must be true to the cause I serve. The great God knows with what sadness I go about this service and with what a perfect hatred I detest this war without an enemy.'

Sir William Waller, 1643

SCOTLAND

Tippermuir 1644 ✕

Dunbar 1650 ✕

Edinburgh ●

Philiphaugh 1645 ✕

Marston Moor 1644 ✕

Preston 1648 ✕

York ■   Hull ●

Manchester ●   Leeds ●

Drogheda 1649 ✕

IRELAND

Chester ■   **ENGLAND**

Nottingham ■

Wexford 1649 ✕

Naseby 1645 ✕

Worcester 1651 ✕   Edgehill 1642 ✕

WALES   Oxford ■

Gloucester ●

Newbury 1643 ✕

Bristol ●   London ●

Portsmouth ●   Dover ●

Exeter ■

Plymouth ●

☐ Areas that mainly supported the King in 1642

☐ Areas that mainly supported Parliament in 1642

■ Royalist towns

● Parliamentary towns

⛵ Navy for Parliament

✕ Battles

Britain during the Civil War seems to have been divided roughly between areas that supported the King, and areas that supported Parliament. Many parts of Britain saw no fighting at all, and most people did not join the war. The biggest battle – at Marston Moor in 1644 – was fought by about 30,000 people.

● *Where was the fighting concentrated?*

Source D

Sir George Sondes was a landowner. He took no part in the fighting. Here, he explains why.

'I had promised my loyalty to the King, but I was never so great a Royalist as to forget that I was a freeborn Englishman. I wanted the King, but not as a tyrant. I wanted to cut the power of the King's advisers. But when it came to King against Parliament, I did not know what to do. As long as I live I will try honestly to have peace with all men. I have suffered because my lands have been seized, but I never acted against anyone.'

Sir George Sondes, 1650

The King's side

- ◆ Noblemen and their servants
- ◆ Supporters of the Church of England
- ◆ Catholics
- ◆ The Irish
- ◆ Poorer areas

Source E

Jonathan Langley was a merchant in Shrewsbury. Most people in that town supported Parliament. Jonathan said he would not join any side, but his neighbours thought that secretly he supported the King.

'I did not want to fight on either side as I am loyal to both King and Parliament. I know there are two armies, each trying to destroy the other and each claiming to be fighting for religion. What reason have I to fall out with either? I want to live at home, in peace.'

Jonathan Langley, 1643

Parliament's side

- ◆ The Scots
- ◆ London
- ◆ The navy
- ◆ Puritans
- ◆ Gentlemen, merchants and townspeople

---

1 According to the map, where was support for Parliament the strongest?

2 Use the information in this unit to help you decide which side each of the following people would have fought on in the Civil War:
- ◆ a London merchant
- ◆ a Lancashire nobleman
- ◆ the nobleman's servant
- ◆ a farmer with a small farm in Suffolk
- ◆ a Puritan preacher from London
- ◆ a merchant in York
- ◆ a farmer with a small farm outside York.

3 a What reasons can you find to explain why some people took part in the Civil War?
b What different reasons can you find in Sources B–E to explain why some people did not want to take part in the Civil War?
c Why does William Waller call the war 'this war without an enemy' (Source C)? Both Waller and Henry Slingsby took part in the war even though they did not want to fight. What clues can you find in Waller's letter that explain this?

4 Sources B–E were all written by men from a rich background. Why do you think it is much more difficult to find out about what ordinary people thought about the war? Look again at the sources in Units 5, 6 and 7 to see if there is any evidence about whether ordinary people actually cared about the argument between the King and Parliament.

8

Why did Parliament win?

Most people in 1642 expected the King to win the Civil War. But they were wrong. After four years of fighting, Parliament was victorious.

Why did Parliament win?

Think about what factors help one side to win in a war. Is it always the side with the most forces that wins?

You might be able to suggest some reasons why Parliament won the war. Perhaps Parliament had better soldiers, or better generals, or more luck. What other reasons might help to explain why Parliament won?

Source A

Oliver Cromwell (1599–1658), Parliamentarian leader

Oliver Cromwell was a country landowner and MP. There is no evidence that he had ever been a soldier before 1642, but he became the outstanding commander of the Civil War. He commanded cavalry regiments, and his daring attacks made him famous. He criticised lords who did not like the idea of fighting the King. Together with Sir Thomas Fairfax he formed the New Model Army in 1645.

What difference did the generals make?

At first, it seemed that no one was really prepared to fight. Parliament's army was commanded by members of the House of Lords who did not like the idea of fighting the King. Charles himself turned out to be a poor commander who was bad at making decisions. As time went on, more important commanders emerged. How good were they?

Source B

Prince Rupert of the Rhine (1619–82), Royalist leader

Rupert was Charles I's nephew. Although he was only 23 in 1642, he had fought in wars in Germany and he was an experienced cavalry commander. Charles relied on him a lot. But Rupert often made decisions without thinking. In important battles like Marston Moor and Naseby, for example, he allowed his cavalry to charge out of control.

Organisation, pay and training

The first battles of the Civil War were more like street fights than battles. No one expected the war to last long, and so no one had really thought about feeding and paying the soldiers. At Marston Moor in 1644, Royalist supplies were so low that the soldiers had to drink water from ditches.

Cromwell and Sir Thomas Fairfax soon realised that if the King was to be beaten, they would have to form a well-trained army. In 1645 they set up the New Model Army. All Parliament's forces were now reorganised into a well-disciplined 'New Model'. The New Model Army was very important in winning the major Battle of Naseby in 1645.

If you look back at the map on page 26, you can see that Parliament controlled London and the richest parts of England. They could afford to pay their soldiers. Cromwell made sure that his New Model Army was paid on time. Charles hoped that other kings in Europe would come to help him, but they never did.

● *Which do you think is more important for an army – discipline or enthusiasm? What other qualities are important?*

Source C

One of the main problems facing armies was the shortage of money. One Royalist officer complained:

'Lack of pay eats through the iron doors of discipline and causes whole armies to rush into disorders.'

Anonymous

Fighting for a cause

Most people thought the King would win because many of his supporters were gentlemen who owned their own weapons and horses. But as we have seen, many of these people did not want to fight.

The setting up of the New Model Army was very important. Cromwell and Fairfax recruited people who disliked Charles because of his religion and his advisers. Most were strongly Puritan, and believed that God was on their side.

Source D

Cromwell promoted men for their ability and loyalty and not because they were rich or noble.

'I had rather have a plain russet-coated captain who knows what he fights for and loves what he knows than that which you call a gentleman but is nothing else.'

Oliver Cromwell, 1645

Support from other countries

Charles believed that once the war started, other kings in Europe would send him money and soldiers. He was disappointed when no one seemed prepared to help him out. On the other hand, Parliament's armies were supported by the Scots in the first years of the war. The Scots had still not forgiven Charles for trying to force the English prayerbook on them in 1639.

Trayle your Pike.   Recover your Pike and Charge. The 1.ᵗ Palming motion.

The 2.ᵈ Palming motion.   Charge your Pike.

Source E
'Exercise of the pike'. These pictures are taken from a training manual dated 1645, written for the New Model Army. The Army was the first full-time, professional and paid army in Britain since the Roman army had left over twelve centuries earlier.

---

1 These were some of the reasons why Parliament won the war:

◆ Parliament had better generals.
◆ The King was a bad decision-maker.
◆ Parliament's soldiers were better trained.
◆ The New Model Army believed in what they were fighting for.
◆ The King's soldiers were not paid regularly.
◆ Parliament controlled the richest parts of Britain.
◆ The Scots supported Parliament.
a Can you find another reason?
b Draw up a table like the one below. Fill it in, putting the reasons in order from most important to least important.

2 Decide whether you think Parliament would have won if:
a they had not had Oliver Cromwell
b they had not controlled the South East
c the New Model Army had not been set up.
Explain your answers.

3 Use the information in this unit, and any other information you can find about the Civil War, to help you write the script for a radio documentary on why Parliament won the Civil War.

4 Does the information in this unit explain fully why Parliament won? If not, what other things do you think might have helped Parliament?

Reason	Why it was important
1	
2	
3	

9

Weapons and tactics: Naseby 1645

The Battle of Naseby decided the outcome of the Civil War.

How can we be sure about what happened there?

In the heat of battle

On a hot June day in 1645, the two armies faced each other across a valley at Naseby in Northamptonshire. Parliament's main army was commanded by Sir Thomas Fairfax and reinforced by Oliver Cromwell and the New Model Army. Facing them were Charles I and Prince Rupert with the Royalist army. Charles had fewer men, but he expected 3,000 more cavalry to arrive during the day. By the end of the day, Charles was beaten. How did it happen?

Some of the soldiers who fought in the battle wrote down their memories of it.

Source A

'The King saw that General Fairfax had arranged his army on the hill. They had also lined up musketeers behind a hedge on our right to fire on our cavalry. Prince Rupert led our cavalry on a charge up the hill. Many were wounded by shots from the hedge before we reached the cavalry. But we drove them back. If we had done as well elsewhere, we might have won the battle. But Rupert chased them too far. Our other cavalry were attacked by the enemy and we were forced to run, leaving all our supplies and baggage.'

Sir Henry Slingsby, 1651

Source B

'We met them early in the morning. They had a large army of 15,000 men, and we had no more than 12,000. They waited for us to attack. We did, and our cavalry on the left were pushed back, but those under Prince Rupert chased the enemy off the hill. As Rupert turned back, General Cromwell's cavalry attacked him. So in effect all our cavalry were chased away. All this time, our infantry battled it out. But they got no help from our cavalry and they were surrounded by Cromwell's cavalry until they were forced to surrender. Fewer than 20 were killed.'

Lord John Belasye, 1654

Source C

'When Prince Rupert drove back our cavalry on the left, we gave ourselves up for lost men, but we decided to fight to the last. And our right wing which was Colonel Cromwell's drove the enemy before them and attacked their infantry. He took 500 prisoners. Then my regiment charged the King's own men and we chased them off towards Leicester.'

Colonel John Okey, 1646

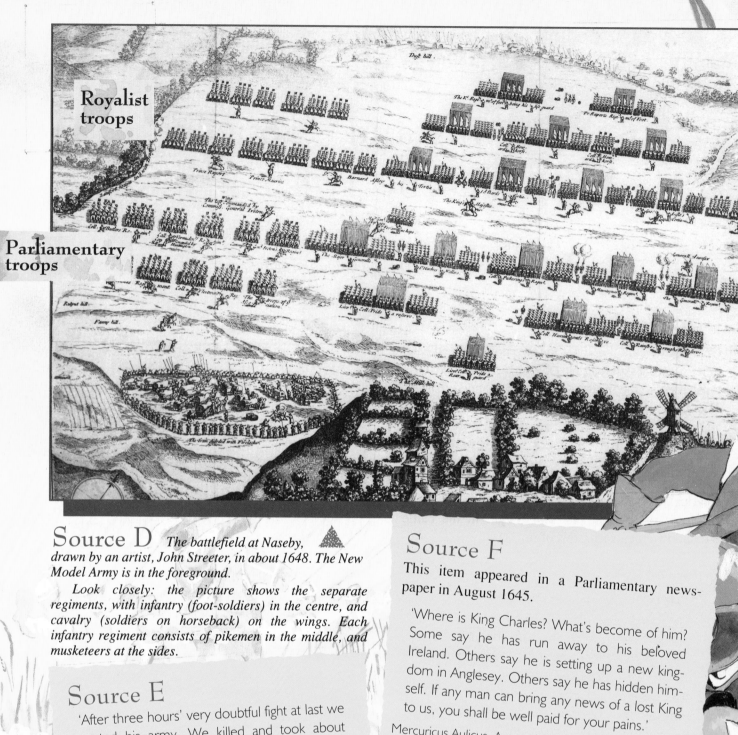

Royalist troops

Parliamentary troops

Source D
The battlefield at Naseby, drawn by an artist, John Streeter, in about 1648. The New Model Army is in the foreground.

Look closely: the picture shows the separate regiments, with infantry (foot-soldiers) in the centre, and cavalry (soldiers on horseback) on the wings. Each infantry regiment consists of pikemen in the middle, and musketeers at the sides.

Source E

'After three hours' very doubtful fight at last we routed his army. We killed and took about 5,000 prisoners and all his guns. We chased the enemy for twelve miles, as far as Leicester where the King fled. Sir, this is none other but the hand of God on our side.'

Oliver Cromwell, 1645

Source F

This item appeared in a Parliamentary news-paper in August 1645.

'Where is King Charles? What's become of him? Some say he has run away to his beloved Ireland. Others say he is setting up a new kingdom in Anglesey. Others say he has hidden himself. If any man can bring any news of a lost King to us, you shall be well paid for your pains.'

Mercuricus Aulicus, August 1645

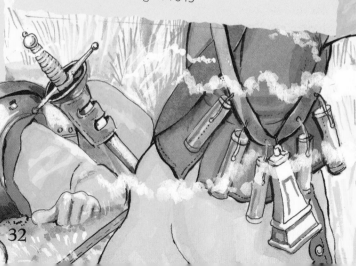

1 a The authors of Sources A–C and E–F all took part in the battle. Can you work out which side each one was on?

b What information can you get from Source D that is not in the written sources? How reliable do you think Source D is?

2 The written accounts of Naseby may seem confusing. Try to work out what happened in the battle by copying and completing the table.
Now use your table to work out the answers to these questions:

◆ Which army was in the better position?
◆ Which was the bigger army?
◆ How successful was Prince Rupert's attack?
◆ What part did Cromwell play in the battle?
◆ Who won? How big was the victory?

3 What mistakes did the King make? What evidence is there that the Parliamentary commanders thought they were lucky?

4 What three pieces of advice would you have given Charles to help the Royalists to win the battle?

	Details	Sources that give information
The position of the armies		
The size of the two armies		
Prince Rupert's charge		
Cromwell's counter-attack		
The end of the battle		

The King is executed

In 1648 Charles I was captured by Parliament. No one trusted him, but Parliament did not really know what to do with him. Eventually they decided to put him on trial. In January 1649, he was put to death.

Why was the King killed? How did people react to the execution?

The trial

Source A

Here, Charles claims that Parliament has no right to put him on trial. It is quite a difficult piece, so read it carefully.

'I demand to know by what power I am called here. By what lawful authority? Remember, I am your King, your lawful King. Think about these things before you go from one sin to a greater one. I have a trust committed to me by God, by lawful inheritance. I will not give it up to answer to a new and unlawful authority.'

Charles I, 1649

● How many times does Charles use the world 'lawful'? Why do you think he uses it so often?

Source B

Parliament went ahead with the trial. This was the verdict.

'Charles Stuart, King of England, trusted to rule according to the laws of this land, had a wicked plan to create for himself an unlimited and unjust power to rule as he wanted.

Like a traitor he waged a war against Parliament and the people. So he is responsible for all the murders, burnings, damage and destruction caused during the war. He is a tyrant, traitor, murderer and an enemy of the people of England.'

Sentence at the High Court of Justice, 1649

● Find out exactly what the word 'traitor' means. Could Charles have been a traitor?

Source C

A modern historian writes about the trial of Charles I.

'If Charles had pleaded "not guilty" he would have been given lawyers. They would have taken up time working out how to defend him. Other kings in Europe would have come to help. Law and order in England would have broken down. But Charles just allowed his accusers to go ahead.'

John Kenyon, *The Civil Wars of England*, 1988

● Why do you think Charles refused to plead not guilty?

Source D
Part of Charles's death warrant. Among the many signatures, can you spot Oliver Cromwell's?

Source E   *In January 1649, Charles I was executed outside the Royal Banqueting Hall in Whitehall, London.*

● *Why do you think he was executed here?*

Source F

These words were spoken by Charles to the people near him just before he died.

'I want the people's freedom as much as anyone, but I must tell you that freedom means having a government and laws.... It does not mean the people having a share in government.'

Charles I, 1649

Source G

An eye-witness wrote this account of the execution.

'I was in the crowd in the street before Whitehall Gate where the scaffold was, and saw what was done, but was not so near as to hear anything. I saw the blow given. At that moment, I remember, there was such a groan from the crowd as I never heard before and hope I may never hear again. There was, as ordered, one troop of soldiers immediately marching to scatter the people, so I had to move quickly to get home without hurt.'

Philip Henry, 1650s

Source H

This extract is taken from a letter which Charles I wrote to his son – who later became Charles II – just before he died.

'I would not have you disliking Parliaments, which in the right place will not reduce your greatness but will give you love, loyalty and confidence.'

Charles I, 1649

Source I

Just after Charles was executed, the remaining MPs in Parliament decided to rule without a king. This is what they said.

'A king is unnecessary. It is dangerous to the freedom and safety of the people. The King has attacked his people and made them poor. No single person shall have the power or title of a king.'

Parliament, 1649

Source J

This needlework was made more than ten years after the execution, in the 1660s. The King's foot is resting on a model of the world. He is shown praying with the Bible open in front of him. Charles's crown is lying on the ground. God has sent a crown of flowers to replace it.

● *Why do you think this needlework was made?*

---

1 a What was Charles I accused of?
b How did he answer the charges against him at his trial (Source A) and at his execution (Source F)?
c Could Charles I have saved himself?

2 Work in pairs.
◆ One of you is a lawyer who is defending Charles I. Write a speech which you could make before Parliament explaining why you think Charles was not guilty.
◆ The other is a lawyer prosecuting Charles. Write a speech which you could make explaining why you think he was guilty.

3 Look at Sources E and G. What do they tell us about the execution?

4 Are you surprised by what Charles wrote about Parliament to his son (Source H)?

5 What did the maker of Source J think about Charles I? Look at what Charles is holding, at the sky, the globe, and his position.

6 Parliament said that Charles was wicked, and executed him. After his death, some people thought of him as a saint. Do you agree with either of these views? Explain your answer in detail.

11

Oliver Cromwell: dictator?

After Charles I had been executed, there was a problem: how should England be ruled? For four years, Parliament tried to rule England. But by 1653, Parliament was unpopular. Then Oliver Cromwell and the army took over. Cromwell became Lord Protector of England.

Had Cromwell always planned to rule England?

Cromwell comes to power

In 1649, Parliament did not stop at executing Charles I. They went on to abolish the Monarchy, the Church of England and the House of Lords. They promised to bring changes in the law and in landowning. But by 1653 very few changes had been made. Parliament was unpopular, taxes were high and Britain was at war with The Netherlands. In April 1653, while Parliament was meeting, Oliver Cromwell arrived at the House of Commons.

Source A

Edmund Ludlow was a Parliamentary leader. During the 1650s he wrote a diary. Here he describes what happened.

'General Cromwell stepped into the middle of the House, and said: "Come, I will put an end to your chatter. You are no Parliament." Then the sergeant attending the Parliament opened the doors and two lines of soldiers entered the House, and ordered the members away.'

Edmund Ludlow, 1653

Source B
The pattern for a coin with Cromwell's head. It was made in 1656, but was never used as money.

● *Can you draw any conclusions about Cromwell from this coin?*

Cromwell made himself 'Lord Protector' of England. This meant that he ruled the country. In 1656 some people asked him to make himself King. Although he did not agree to call himself King, he certainly behaved like one: he called Parliaments to meet, and asked them to vote taxes and to make laws.

Did Cromwell want to be King? Sources C and D offer two opinions. Sources D, F and G will help you to decide.

Source C

'Cromwell wanted very much to be the king.'
Edmund Ludlow, 1650

37

Source D

This is what Cromwell said about himself.

'I did not push myself into this position, of that God be my witness. I could not refuse the power God put into my hands.'

Oliver Cromwell, 1656

● Should we believe what Cromwell said about himself?

Source F

Edward Hyde was a supporter of Charles I and he became one of Charles II's ministers. He wrote his own history of the Civil War.

'Cromwell was the greatest liar alive. He did great mischief, but he had courage, and worked hard. Without any doubt, no man ever tried anything with more wickedness, but even his wickedness had a great spirit. He forced three countries that hated him to obey his commands, and he ruled with an army that was devoted to him.'

Edward Hyde, 1664

Source G

Samuel Pepys kept a diary from 1660 to 1669. In it he describes what people thought of Cromwell.

'Everybody do nowadays talk about Oliver and praise him, what brave things he did, making foreign countries fear him.'

Samuel Pepys, 1667

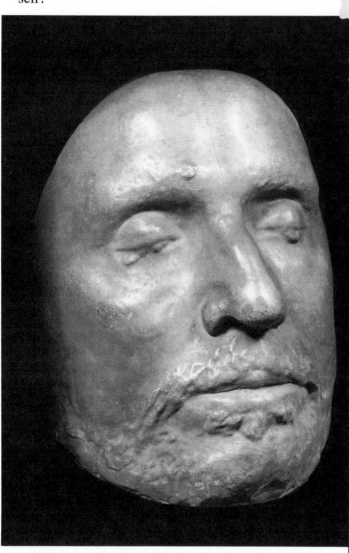

Source E *The death mask of Oliver Cromwell. From being a Cambridgeshire landowner and MP, Cromwell became ruler of all Britain between 1653 and 1658. He was a strong Puritan, a brilliant general and a very efficient organiser.*

1 What different ideas can you pick out from Sources A, C and D about why Cromwell became Lord Protector?

2 Cromwell said that he never wanted to become Lord Protector (Source D). Does this *prove* that he did not want to be Lord Protector?

3 a What image of Cromwell does Source B give you?
b How does this affect your attitude to what Cromwell said in Source D?

4 a What evidence can you find in this unit that ideas about Cromwell changed as time went on?
b Why do you think people's ideas about Cromwell changed?
c A new encyclopedia is being written. The editor wants a forty-word entry on Oliver Cromwell. Use the information in this unit to write an entry.

Cromwell in Ireland

In 1649 there was a rebellion in Ireland in support of Charles I's son. Parliament sent Oliver Cromwell and an army to defeat the rebels. All over Ireland, Cromwell won battles and restored order. But his fierce campaign has caused argument ever since.

How can we explain what Cromwell did in Ireland? Was he a hero or a murderer?

Rebellion in Ireland

Ireland was a largely Catholic country. Many Irish Catholics had been fighting for the King since 1641. After Charles I was executed, Parliament worried that his supporters would launch an attack from Ireland.

Rebellion broke out against Parliament and spread all over Ireland. There were reports that the rebels had massacred Protestant women and children during the war. Cromwell was sent with 3,000 well-trained soldiers to end the rebellion and to punish those people responsible for the massacres. Cromwell's troops defeated rebels all over Ireland. After a quick campaign, Cromwell's army surrounded the rebel stronghold at Drogheda. He asked the rebels to surrender, but it was more than two weeks before they did so.

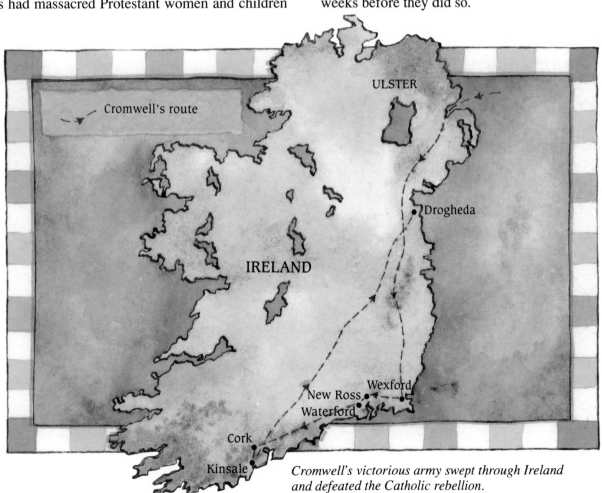

Cromwell's victorious army swept through Ireland and defeated the Catholic rebellion.

39

Source A

Cromwell's assault on Drogheda. Here his army massacred men, women and children.

Source B

Cromwell wrote a letter to the House of Commons reporting the attack on Drogheda. Cromwell's troops had burst through the walls. He explains what happened next and goes on to try to explain why he acted in this way.

'Many of the enemy retreated to Mill Mount – a very strong and difficult place to attack. The Governor, Sir Arthur Ashton, and many important officers were there, and our men were ordered by me to kill them all.

Indeed in the heat of the action I told them not to spare anyone they found armed. I think they killed about 2,000 men.

The next day they fought still, and killed and wounded some of our men. When hunger forced them to surrender, their officers were knocked on the head and every tenth man of the soldiers was killed; the rest were shipped away as slaves.

I believe that this is God's judgement on these barbarous wretches who have massacred innocent Protestants. It will prevent any trouble in the future. This explains what we did, which of course makes us both sad and sorry. The officers and soldiers of this garrison were the best of their army. They hoped that our attempt to capture this place would ruin us.

Some of us believe that a great thing like this can only be done if God is on our side. It was Him who gave our men courage, and this happy success. And therefore God should have all the glory.'

Oliver Cromwell, 1650

Sources C and D present the views of two modern historians.

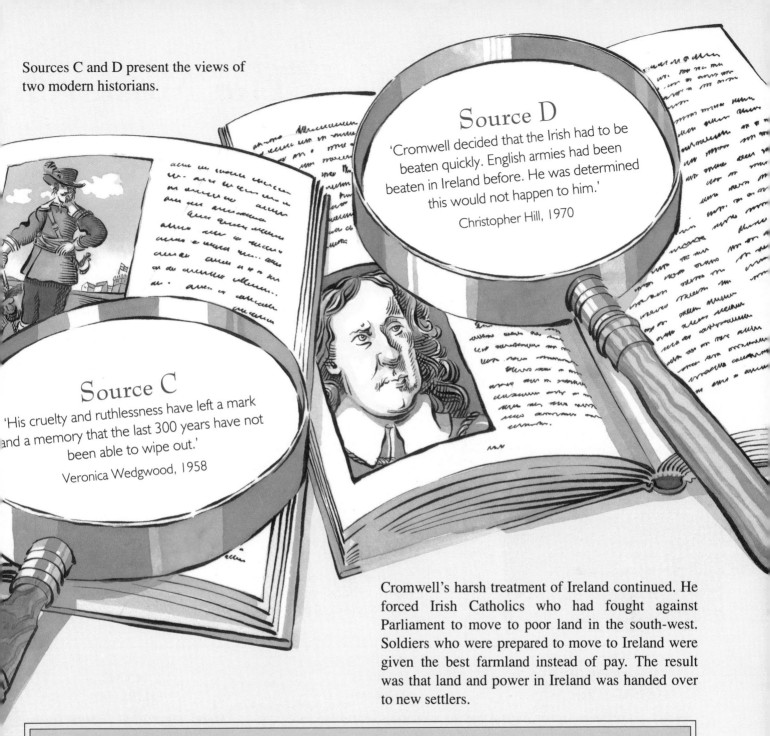

Source D

'Cromwell decided that the Irish had to be beaten quickly. English armies had been beaten in Ireland before. He was determined this would not happen to him.'

Christopher Hill, 1970

Source C

'His cruelty and ruthlessness have left a mark and a memory that the last 300 years have not been able to wipe out.'

Veronica Wedgwood, 1958

Cromwell's harsh treatment of Ireland continued. He forced Irish Catholics who had fought against Parliament to move to poor land in the south-west. Soldiers who were prepared to move to Ireland were given the best farmland instead of pay. The result was that land and power in Ireland was handed over to new settlers.

1 Why did the defenders of Drogheda surrender? What happened to them when they did?

2 What reasons did Cromwell give to explain what he had done?

3 Look at Sources A and B carefully.
◆ Make a list of all the evidence that supports Veronica Wedgwood's view of Cromwell.
◆ Make a list of all the evidence that supports Christopher Hill's view of Cromwell.
This can be done in the form of a table:

Evidence supporting Veronica Wedgwood's view	Evidence supporting Christopher Hill's view

4 Why do you think historians like Wedgwood and Hill disagree about Cromwell? What do *you* think about Cromwell?

This is the 'family tree' of the kings and queens who ruled between 1603 and 1760. The dates given show the length of each monarch's reign.

CHARLES I
(1625–49; executed)

In 1642, a civil war broke out between Charles and Parliament. Charles lost the war, and was executed in 1649.

Mary

CHARLES II
(1660–85)

In 1658 Oliver Cromwell died. There was no-one strong enough to take his place. In 1660 Charles II was welcomed back to England as King. But within seven years he was unpopular. He had promised to rule with Parliament's help, but lost patience and tried to rule alone.

The revolution of 1688
By 1688 one group of politicians were so worried about James II that they decided to replace him. They asked a Dutch Protestant, Prince William of Orange, to bring an army to Britain. It was not needed, because James II ran away.

Bill of Rights
William III and Mary II became joint King and Queen after 1688. In the Bill of Rights they promised to let Parliament look after most of the government of the country.

Whigs and Tories
Politicians who believed that Parliament, rather than the King, should control taxes, government and the army were nicknamed 'Whigs'. Supporters of royal power were called 'Tories'.

WILLIAM III   =   MARY II
(1688–1702)   (1688–94)

An Act of Parliament made William and his wife Mary joint rulers in 1688, and made it illegal for Catholics to inherit the throne. William and Mary agreed that Parliament controlled taxes, and gave permission for the King to command the army. Mary left government to William.

ANNE
(1701–14)

Mary's sister Anne became Queen, but left government business to her ministers in Parliament. All her children were stillborn or died as children. There was no obvious successor.

is restored

JAMES I
(1603–25; James VI of Scots 1567–1625)

James was King of Scotland and King of England. There were arguments over money, power and religion during his reign. In 1625 his son, Charles, succeeded.

Elizabeth

Sophia

JAMES II
(1685–88)

James was Charles II's brother and a Catholic. Some of the things he did reminded people of Charles I.

James
('the Old Pretender')

James II took his baby son, also called James, with him to France. In 1715 James 'the Old Pretender' came to Scotland with an army to try to take the Crown from George I. Many people in Scotland supported him, but he failed.

GEORGE I
(1714–27)

Eventually Parliament invited a distant cousin of Anne to become king. George I ruled a small German state called Hanover. He did not speak any English.

GEORGE II
(1727–60)

Like his father, George II was not interested in ruling Britain, and left things to Parliament. Under George I and George II, Britain became one of the most powerful countries in Europe.

13

Charles II and the Restoration

In September 1658 Oliver Cromwell died. In May 1660, Charles I's son, Charles II, came back to England as King. He was welcomed by cheering crowds in London. The Monarchy was now restored.

Twenty years later, a group of politicians tried to overthrow Charles II. Why did things go wrong?

A new King

When Charles II became King, there were many questions to be sorted out. How were they settled?

✷ What would happen to the Church?

Charles II promised to support the Church of England, but to allow different religions. In fact Charles was secretly a Catholic, and he tried to punish Protestants.

✷ What would happen to people who had fought against Charles I?

Most were pardoned. Those who actually signed Charles I's death warrant were killed. The bodies of Cromwell and other leaders were dug up and beheaded.

✷ Would the King rule with or without Parliament?

Charles II promised to rule with the help of Parliament. He was given an income to rely on. In fact he spent a lot of money, and tried to find ways of getting round Parliament.

✷ Could the King be trusted?

Charles said he could. But he made a secret treaty with France (a Catholic country) in which he promised to help them in a war. He never told Parliament about this.

Source A

After Cromwell died, no one seemed to be able to control Parliament or the army. In 1660, a group of generals asked Charles II to become King. John Evelyn, a supporter of Charles II, saw the Restoration procession.

'He came with over 20,000 followers, waving their swords with joy. The ways were covered with flowers, the bells were ringing, the streets were hung with tapestries and the fountains ran with wine . . . And all this was done without any bloodshed, by the very army that rebelled against his father.'

John Evelyn, 1660

Plots against the King

Charles II did not behave in the way people thought he would. Within a few years, some people wished he had never become King. After 1667 his opponents tried to plot against him. A group of Protestant politicians, nicknamed the Whigs, tried to pass laws in Parliament to control Charles. In 1679 they tried to pass a law that would stop Charles's Catholic brother becoming King. When Charles dismissed Parliament, the Whigs thought he was behaving like his father.

Some of them organised a secret plot to take over England. It failed, and they had to escape abroad. But twenty years after the Restoration, England seemed to be as divided as it had been before. Was it all Charles's fault?

Source B *The Restoration of Charles II in 1660. The procession
moves from the Tower of London to Westminster. This late seventeenth-century
painting is by a Dutch artist, Dirck Stoop.*

Source C   *The new King's supporters took revenge on those who had executed Charles I. The bodies of Cromwell and other leaders were dug up, hung and beheaded.*

Inset: The head of Oliver Cromwell is believed to be buried under the chapel of Sidney Sussex College in Cambridge.

Some views on Charles II

Source D

David Hume was a Scottish historian. This piece is taken from a history book that he wrote a hundred years after Charles II died.

'He ignored what was good for Britain, and he did not like Britain's religion. He spent its treasure. But he was guided by his moods, and by his love for France.'

David Hume, 1767

Source E

The man who wrote this was made a bishop by Charles II.

'He could be charming with anyone, but they could not tell when he was pleased or not. He was a chatterbox, who understood science well. He disguised the fact that he was a Catholic until he died. And he thought that any king who could be controlled by Parliament was not really a king.'

Gilbert Burnet, 1690

---

1 Look again at Sources A and B. What image did Charles want to give at his Restoration?

2 Was Charles a good king? Using the sources in this unit, list what you think were his good and bad qualities.

3 a Look again at the whole of this unit. Make two lists to show:

◆ all those things that *Charles and his supporters* did which led to argument and disagreement

◆ all those things that *Charles's opponents* did which led to argument and disagreement.

b Now explain whether you think that the disagreements of Charles II's reign were his fault or not.

14

1688: year of revolution

James II became King in 1685. He promoted Catholics at court and in the army. This made him very unpopular with many Protestant politicians. In 1688 they asked the Protestant prince, William of Orange, to invade. James escaped to France. William and Mary became the new rulers. This dramatic change is sometimes called 'the glorious revolution'.

Why did William win so easily?

The Catholic King

James II did not trust Parliament or the Church. He sent Parliament away and made his own laws. As a result he became very unpopular. Many people thought that he was trying to copy the things that Charles I had done before 1642. But James was 52 and had no son. He knew he was getting old and would not be King for long.

Then in June 1688, James's second wife, Mary, gave birth to a son. The son, also called James, would grow up as a Catholic and would become the next King. The Whigs decided to act. Seven leading politicians turned for help to William of Orange, the ruler of the Netherlands, who was married to James's daughter.

Was William lucky?

William set sail for England on 19 October 1688. He planned to land in the east, where James had an army and navy waiting, but he was blown off course, and his ships were swept down the English Channel. When he landed in Devon he met no opposition.

Source A

Seven politicians sent this secret message to William on 30 June 1688.

'The people are so unhappy with what the king has done about religion and freedom that nineteen out of twenty of them want a change. The nobility are just as unhappy, though it is not safe to talk to many of them. Some of the most important lords would join you as soon as you landed in England.'

Government papers, released in 1700

Source B

John Evelyn recorded the events of that autumn 1688 in his diary.

5 November I went to London. Heard the news that Prince William had landed at Torbay, a fleet of nearly 700 ships. He sailed through the Channel with so favourable a wind that our navy could not intercept them. This threw King James into great worry.

14 November The Prince becomes more powerful every day. Several lords go to him. The city of London is in disorder.

2 December The King's favourites and his priests run away. Papist officers in the army run away too. It looks like a revolution.

13 December The King runs away to sea, puts in at Faversham for supplies; is attacked by the people, comes back to London.

18 December I saw the King take a boat from London at 12 o'clock – a sad sight! The Prince comes to London and fills the court with Dutch soldiers. All the world go to see the Prince. He is stately, serious and reserved.

Source C *An engraving by a Dutch artist to show William of Orange's arrival in 1688. In the background is London, with crowds of people turning out to welcome William.*

● *Can you find the Prince of Orange in this picture?*

After William's arrival in London, Parliament met. They asked him to be King, but first he had to agree to an important document. This is what it said:

Declaration of Rights 1689

No Catholic can become King.

YES I'M CATHOLIC
THEN YOU CAN'T VOTE
Catholics cannot vote.

Parliament decides on laws and taxes, not the King.

Parliament keeps a check on the army.

1 Look at these events from 1688. Sort them into order and produce a strip cartoon or story board to illustrate them.

William lands in Devon.

James leaves England in a hurry.

Important lords desert James.

James's wife has a son.

Seven politicians invite William to England.

Officers in James's army run away.

2 John Evelyn's diary is a very important historical source for the events of 1688. Read Source B carefully. Note down all the words or phrases where Evelyn seems to express his own opinion. What do you think Evelyn thought about William?

3 In their letter to William, the seven politicians said 'nineteen out of twenty people' would support William (Source A). What other evidence can you find in this unit to back up this view?

4 Source C is a painting of William's arrival in London.
a Do you think it is a painting by a supporter of William or a supporter of James?
b How accurate do you think the source is?

5 The Whigs called the events of 1688 'the glorious revolution'. Why do you think they thought it was 'glorious'?

15

Britain – a United Kingdom?

Some historians believe that between 1500 and 1750 the four nations – England, Wales, Ireland and Scotland – became a 'United Kingdom'.

How united were the British Isles by 1750?

	A United Kingdom or . . .	. . . four nations?
1515		The English army defeats the Scots at the Battle of Flodden.
1536	The English Parliament passes the first Act of Union with Wales.	
1543	The English Parliament passes the final Act of Union with Wales.	
1567		Elizabeth I has Mary Queen of Scots arrested, imprisoned, and later executed in 1587.
1603	The Scottish King, James VI, also becomes James I of England.	
1642 – 1651	The English Civil War involves all of the British Isles: the Irish fight for Charles I, the Scots change sides.	
1660	Restoration of Charles II as King.	
1690	William III establishes English control in Ireland and Scotland. The Irish are defeated at the Battle of the Boyne. The Scottish clans surrender to William.	
1707	The English Parliament passes the Act of Union with Scotland.	
1715		James Edward, the 'Old Pretender', leads a Scottish rebellion.
1745		Bonnie Prince Charlie, the 'Young Pretender', leads a Catholic Scottish rebellion. The rebellion is defeated at the Battle of Culloden.

A United Kingdom? The Tudors and Wales

Between 1536 and 1543, Henry VIII passed two Acts of Union with Wales.

English monarchs had always had problems in controlling the remote, wild parts of Wales. The aim of the Acts was to increase the control the Tudors had in Wales.

The Acts of Union

★ ended the Welsh tradition of dividing land between all the sons when the owner died – land now had to be passed to the eldest son, as in England

★ divided Wales into counties in the same way as England

★ gave Wales MPs in the English Parliament

★ insisted that all people in charge of local government must speak English.

A United Kingdom? The Scottish rebellions

The Act of Union of 1707 brought England and Scotland fully together. The Scots now sent MPs to the English Parliament: the Scottish Parliament met for the last time.

However, many Scots remained unhappy with the government in London. In 1715 and 1745 Scottish armies tried to overthrow the government. On both occasions they were defeated. In 1745 the Scots were massacred at the Battle of Culloden.

Source A

'The road from Culloden was full of dead bodies. The Duke of Cumberland [the English commander] stripped the wounded of their clothes and left them with the dead on the battlefield for two days. Then he sent soldiers to kill those still alive. He ordered a barn with Highlanders in it to be set on fire, and his soldiers drove back any who tried to save themselves from the flames.'

Chevalier de Johnstone, one of Prince Charles's soldiers, 1746

Source B *The English victory at Culloden, 1746. James II's grandson, Bonnie Prince Charlie, was defeated in the battle. The English commander, the Duke of Cumberland, is on horseback at the front of the picture (centre). This print was made by a London man called Carrington Bowles.*

Source C
Fort George, the English stronghold built by William III in Scotland.

- *Why did William need to build a fort like this in Scotland?*

A United Kingdom? The Irish question

Did Ireland become part of the United Kingdom? Like the Scots, the Irish supported the Catholic King James II. William III had taken an army to Ireland in 1690. He only conquered the country after a series of battles, which ended with the Battle of the Boyne in 1690.

William III and the English kings and queens who followed tried to make sure of their control of Ireland. Land was taken away from the Catholic landowners and given to Protestant settlers. Catholics were sent away to the poorest parts of Ireland to farm. Most Irish Catholics remained deeply unhappy about the way they were governed.

Source D
Supporters of the Orange Order marching in Northern Ireland. William of Orange established British control in Ireland in 1690. Today he is still seen as a hero by many Protestants in Northern Ireland. Every year they celebrate the anniversary of the Battle of the Boyne, when William of Orange defeated the Catholics.

The United Kingdom today

Today in Wales, many schools still teach in Welsh. The Scottish system of schooling is still separate and different from that in England. Welsh and Scottish Nationalists still demand some control over their own affairs. They want their own parliaments. In Northern Ireland people still disagree passionately about whether they should be ruled from London. And all four nations have their own sports teams.

One kingdom – or four nations?

● Scottish, Irish and Welsh identities in particular are still strong. Can you think of any other ways in which we are 'four nations'?

Source E   *A rugby international between England and Wales.*

1 The year is 1750. Three strangers meet in a London tavern. They are Irish, Scots and Welsh. As they drink together, they discuss the way in which the English have taken control of each of their countries. Produce a script of their conversation.

2 Here are two views about the 'making' of the United Kingdom:

'Between 1500 and 1750 the four nations of Britain became a United Kingdom.'

Anne Historian, 1990

'Although the English gained more power between 1500 and 1750, Britain was not really united. Even today there is disunity.'

A. Researcher, 1991

a Go through the unit and make a list of all the evidence that supports the first view. Go through again and make a list of the evidence that supports the second view.

b How can you explain the fact that historians still disagree about how united the British Isles became between 1500 and 1750?

The population increases

There was a large increase in population between 1500 and 1750. Many towns grew larger. Forests and waste land which had not been farmed for over 200 years were farmed again, because with more people there was a greater demand for food. Prices went up, and some farmers became very rich.

Britain trades more overseas

Britain traded more and more with other countries. From the fifteenth century, the cloth trade was very important and so sheep farming became more profitable. Later on, trade with more distant lands such as India developed, and new goods were bought and sold.

Some farming land is enclosed

After 1500, richer landowners began to enclose, or fence off, fields for sheep farming. In some areas these enclosures replaced the open field system. Enclosure meant that there could be bigger farms which were often more efficient. Enclosures also meant fewer jobs on farms for ordinary people.

There are more poor people

With more people and fewer jobs, there was an increasing number of poor people. These poor people often relied on begging, and many made their way to towns where they hoped to find work. The government was worried by the increase in begging, and punished beggars.

1500–1750

More people are involved in making things

One way in which people tried to solve the problem of being poor was to find new work. In many poor villages people started new industries at home. Some people made stockings, others made silk, and others produced beer.

Towns become more important

There were more people and so more trade. London was the most important town all through the years between 1500 and 1750, and it seems to have grown faster and bigger than anywhere else in Europe.

New methods of farming are introduced

By 1700, large estates were developing all over Britain. Big profits from farming, trade and industry meant that landowners could afford to build huge country houses. They also set up large farms where more efficient farming methods were developed.

New discoveries are made

The period between 1500 and 1750 was an age of great exploration. Between 1578 and 1580, Sir Francis Drake sailed all round the world. He was the first Englishman to do so. Other explorers visited new lands, searching out new trading routes. By 1750 Britain was the world's leading trading nation.

16

Change in the countryside

Between 1500 and 1750 there were many changes in the countryside.
What caused these changes? What effects did they have?

Increasing population

Source A
1730: Bringing in the harvest at the village of Dixton in Gloucestershire. Everyone is working on the landlord's estate. In the past they might have worked on their own small farms.

● *How many different farming jobs can you see being done?*

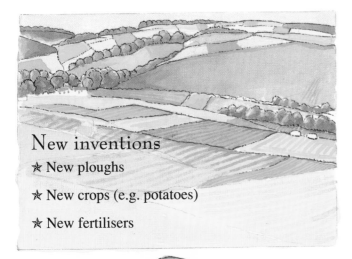

New inventions

* New ploughs

* New crops (e.g. potatoes)

* New fertilisers

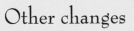

Other changes

* Prices rose

* Rents went up

* People with small farms sold them or left them – some moved to towns

* Large estate farms developed after 1650

New methods

* Enclosing the open fields for sheep

* Flooding the fields for part of the year to make the soil more fertile

* Publication of many books describing better farming methods

1 a Source A gives us some clues about farming in 1730.
* What different jobs did the people in the village have?
* How were animals used to help with the farm work?
* What crops were grown around Dixton?
* What time of year was this picture painted?

b This picture is not a quick sketch. It must have taken the artist a long time to paint.
* Why might it have been painted?
* How would you check that your answer is correct?

2 Look at the drawings in this unit. The changes are all connected.
    What connections do you think there might have been between:
* population increase and rising prices
* enclosure and people leaving the land?

3 Using as many other resources as you can find, write the script for a television documentary about the changes which took place in the countryside between 1500 and 1750.

17
Change in the towns: London

Many towns in Britain became busier and more important between 1500 and 1750. There were more people to feed, and more goods to trade. Towns like Norwich, Bristol and Exeter became more and more important as places to buy and sell things. Smaller towns became centres for trade and industry. In this unit we look at one example: London, the biggest town of all.

How did London change?

Source A
London in about 1620, drawn by a man called Visscher. The Tower of London is in the background, on the right.

- *What information does this picture give us about London?*
- *Look back at the picture of London in about 1500, on page 5. How has the city changed in about a hundred years?*
- *Look at the picture of London in 1710, on page 91. After the Great Fire of London in 1666, much of the city was rebuilt. How did the city change in the next hundred years?*

Source B
This piece is taken from a book about London, written in 1581. Unfortunately we do not know anything about the author.

'The size of London and its need for food not only provides work for farmers and shopkeepers for thirty miles around but even as far as eighty miles away. And if London carries on growing, then it will create employment for people much further off.'

John Houghton, 1581

Source C *The population of London, 1500–1750.*

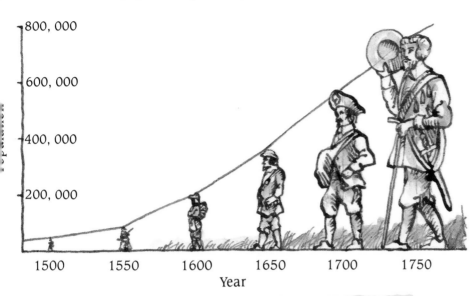

(Graph: Population axis marked 200,000 / 400,000 / 600,000 / 800,000; Year axis marked 1500, 1550, 1600, 1650, 1700, 1750)

Source E

Sir Philip Hoby was an English diplomat who travelled all over Europe.

'London is a stinking city, the filthiest in all the world.'

Philip Hoby, 1578

Source F

This is taken from a book about good manners written in 1579.

'The habit of most gentlemen and noblemen is to house themselves in the suburbs of the city of London, because most commonly the places are healthy and we have as little to fear from diseases as in the countryside.'

Civil and Uncivil Life, 1579

Source D

An Italian visitor expressed his opinion of England's cities in 1588.

'In England, excepting London, there is not one city that deserves to be called great.'

Giovanni Botero, 1588

---

1 Look at Source A.
a How could you use this evidence to suggest that
◆ London was crowded
◆ the river was very important to London
◆ farming was important to London?
b How many churches can you see? Does that mean that people at the time were very religious?
c What other information about London can you find from this piece of evidence?

2 Use all the evidence in this unit to complete a table showing the good and the bad things about living in London in the sixteenth century.

3 a Suggest two things that you can find out from Source A but not from any of the written evidence.

b Suggest two things that you can find out from the written evidence but not from Source A.
c How does the picture help to support the written evidence?

4 a Which of the sources in this unit tell you about the growth of London?
b Besides growing, find three other ways in which London was changing.

5 What evidence can you find in the sources that London was probably not typical of all English towns?

Do you think there are any ways in which the history of London might help to tell us about other towns?

18

The lives of the poor

There were big differences between rich and poor people in Britain between 1500 and 1750.
What can we find out about the lives of poor people?

What evidence is there?

Most of the evidence historians have about the past is about rich people. Not many poor people could write, and their houses have not survived. So it is difficult for historians to find out what life was like for poor people, or even how many poor people there were. Instead, historians have to piece together different types of evidence. This unit is based on some of the different types of evidence that exist. What can they tell us about poor people?

● Why do you think the houses of the rich have survived, but not the houses of the poor?

Source B *A print of a beggar, sixteenth century.*
● *Why do you think very few pictures of beggars were produced?*

Source A *A shepherd working in an enclosed field.*

Source C

In 1522 the government taxed everyone in England according to how much they owned. This table gives you the figures for three villages in Suffolk, and one large town in the West Midlands.

Value of goods (£)	Number of people in each wealth group in			
	Lavenham	Nayland	Sudbury	Coventry
Nil	23	28	43	699
1–9	76	73	127	494
10–99	46	81	32	164
100–499	10	4	8	17
500–999	1	0	0	1
1,000 and over	1	0	0	2

W. G. Hoskins, *The Age of Plunder*, 1978

● What taxes do people pay in Britain today?

Source D

Norwich Council was very worried about the number of poor people in the city. In 1570, they carried out a survey of the poor. These are three examples of poor people.

- Ann Buckle, aged 46, widow, who teaches children and has two children, one aged 5 and one 9, who both work lace. They have always lived here.

- John Burr, 54 years old, very sick and not in work, and Alice his wife, who spins. They have seven children, the eldest 20, the others 12, 10, 8, 6, 4 and one of 2 years that can spin wool.

- John Findlay, 82 years old, not in work, and Joan his wife, sick, who spins and knits.'

Norwich Records, 1570

Source E

Monks and nuns often looked after poor and sick people. Between 1536 and 1539 all the monasteries in England and Wales were closed down by Henry VIII. Monasteries in Scotland and Ireland were destroyed later.

In 1536 there was a rebellion in the North called 'The Pilgrimage of Grace'. Robert Aske, its leader, gave one of the reasons for it.

'We object to the closing down of the monasteries because they gave help to poor men and served God. There is no help for the poor now.'

Robert Aske's confession, 1537

Source F

There were laws about what should happen to poor people who started begging. This is a description of what happened to one beggar in Yorkshire.

'A woman of Hutton Rudby, being a wandering beggar, is to be whipped by the constables of Thirsk and sent on to the next constable to be whipped and so from constable to constable to Rudby.'

Yorkshire Court Records, 1657

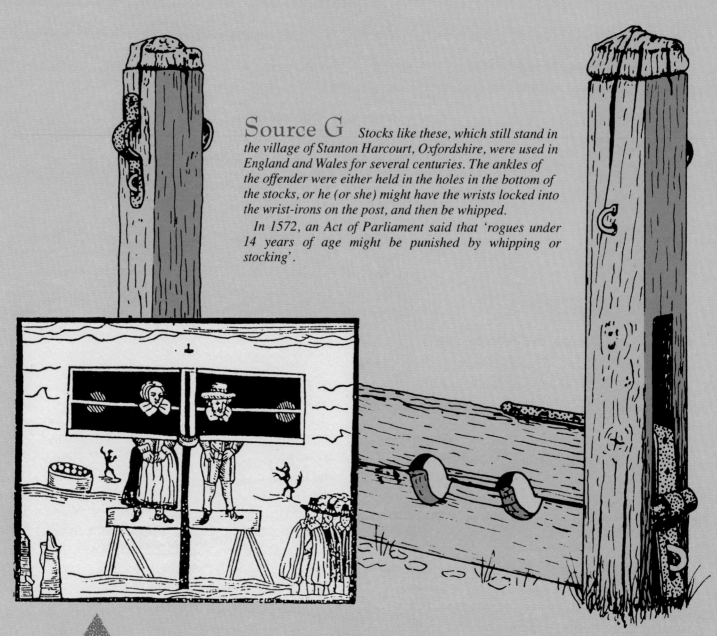

Source G *Stocks like these, which still stand in the village of Stanton Harcourt, Oxfordshire, were used in England and Wales for several centuries. The ankles of the offender were either held in the holes in the bottom of the stocks, or he (or she) might have the wrists locked into the wrist-irons on the post, and then be whipped.*

In 1572, an Act of Parliament said that 'rogues under 14 years of age might be punished by whipping or stocking'.

Source H *Two people in the pillory in London in 1613. Persistent beggars might be put in the pillory.*

● *How is the pillory different from the stocks?*

---

1 Which of the sources in this unit give you information about:
◆ the way poor people were treated by the authorities
◆ the way poor people tried to help themselves
◆ the attitude of better-off people to the poor
◆ the differences between town and country
◆ the causes of being poor?

2 a Look at Sources A and B. What can you find out about poor people from these pictures?

b What can you find out from these pictures that you cannot find out from the written sources?

3 a Source C gives you data for four places. Work out on a pie chart or graph a way of presenting these figures. Then decide which of the four places was the richest and which was the poorest.

b How could a historian use a computer to help analyse these figures?

19

The lives of women

Most of the people you have read about in this book were men.

Why is this? What do we know about women between 1500 and 1750?

Hidden from history?

Historians have always found it difficult to find out about the lives of women. Most of the evidence we have used in this book was written by men. Look at Source A. What does it tell us about the way men at the time thought about women?

In this unit you will have the chance to work out how accurately Source A describes the role of women.

Look at all the evidence, and then decide whether you agree or disagree that women spent their time working only in the home.

Source A

This extract was written by a lawyer.

'Nature has made women to look after the home, to nourish their family and children, and not to meddle with other matters, or be on a council, any more than or children.'

Sir Thomas Smith, 1565

Source B *The Saltonstall family in the 1630s. The wife has just had another baby.*

- *Who is shown as the most important member of the group?*
- *How has the artist shown this?*
- *What does this picture suggest is women's main role?*

Source E

A modern historian describes the siege at Lathom House, Lancashire, during the Civil War in the 1640s.

'The Parliamentary army surrounded Lathom House. Inside was Charlotte, Countess of Derby, with a small number of soldiers. She refused to surrender and even counter-attacked her opponents, who outnumbered her. The Countess held out for three months until a Royalist army arrived.'

◢ Source C *A woman at work on a farm in the seventeenth century.*

- *Were there any differences between the work done by men and women?*

Source F

A Norfolk farmer in the seventeenth century writes:

'Judith Carpenter does all types of work. At the harvest she goes every day with the cart to the field and rakes up after the cart. She runs the dairy and gets the birds ready for market. She spins as well, and does as much as anyone else on the farm.'

Parish records from Norfolk, 1615

Source D

A woman in the Civil War during the 1640s. This woodcut of a 'she-souldier' is from the ballad of 'The Valiant Virgin'.

Source G

Some women were involved in business.

'Joan Dant died aged 84, in 1715. She left more than £9,000. She had been married. After her husband died she worked selling cloth. She did business all over England and as far away as Paris and Brussels.'

Antonia Fraser, *The Weaker Vessel*, 1984

---

1 In this unit women are described as doing several different jobs. Make a list of these.

2 Which sources would you use to prove or disprove the following statements?
◆ Women played no part in the Civil War.
◆ Women's work was only in the home.

3 a Does the evidence in this unit suggest that Source A is a fair statement of what women did in the seventeenth century?
b How could you find out more about whether the answer you gave to (a) is right?

20

The family

How can we find out about family life between 1500 and 1750?
Historians have a number of different theories.

How can we test their ideas?

Theory 1: People got married when they were very young

One idea historians have had about families in the past was that people got married when they were very young. For example, in William Shakespeare's play *Romeo and Juliet*, which was written in about 1595, Juliet is only 14 when she prepares to marry. Her mother was married at 13. Many noble and royal children were betrothed (engaged) before their teens.

One historian, Peter Laslett, has investigated this theory to see if this is typical. He looked at church registers. These record all baptisms, marriages and burials of ordinary people in churches from 1538 onwards. This explains what he found.

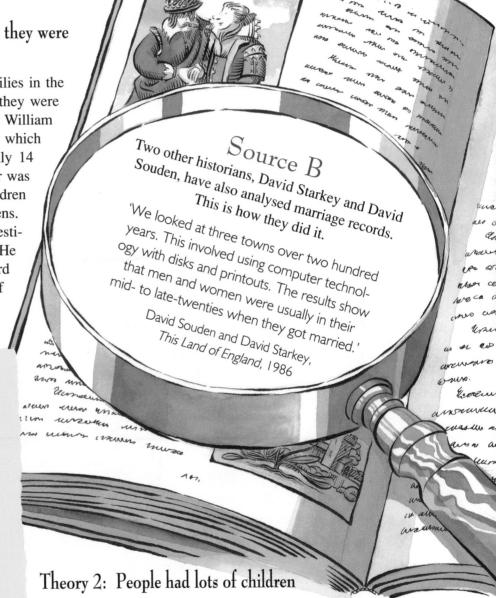

Source B

Two other historians, David Starkey and David Souden, have also analysed marriage records. This is how they did it.

'We looked at three towns over two hundred years. This involved using computer technology with disks and printouts. The results show that men and women were usually in their mid- to late-twenties when they got married.'

David Souden and David Starkey,
This Land of England, 1986

Source A

'All the evidence is that marriage at this age was very rare. Church records show that the commonest age for women to get married was 22 and for men 24.

Some marriages did take place when people were very young. But the church records show that this was only one or two in every thousand, and the evidence showed that older people did not approve. In 1623 a vicar wrote that he had married a man aged 17 to a girl aged 14, and then wrote down "a couple of young fools".'

Peter Laslett, *The World We Have Lost*, 1984 edition.

Theory 2: People had lots of children

Another idea historians have had about families is that people had many children and lived together with lots of different relatives. This is sometimes called 'the extended family'. Pictures like Source D encourage this idea. Again, some research has shown that this idea might be wrong.

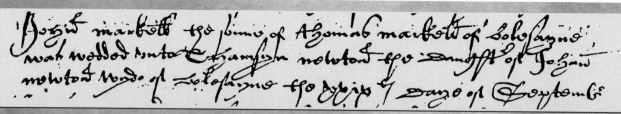

John Markell the sonne of Thomas markell of Bolesayne was wedded vnto Thamsyn Newton the daughter of Johan Newton wydower of Bolesayne the xixth day of September [1579].

John Markel the sonne of Thomas Markle of Bolsayne was christned the iiijth daye of Novembre [1555].

Tamsyn Newton daughter of John Newton of Sladene was christned the xxx daye of Septembre [1556].

Source C
Extracts from some church records. Each extract is explained. The original spelling has been kept.

- *How old do you think John was when he married Tamsyn?*
- *How old do you think Tamsyn was on her wedding day?*
- *What problems do historians face when they study church records of this time?*

Source D
Lord Cobham and his family in 1567. His wife, Lady Frances Cobham, aged 25, is sitting beside him. Her elder sister, Jane, who is probably unmarried, is on the right. The children (from left to right) are: Maximilian (aged 2), Henry (aged 1), William (aged 6), Elizabeth and Frances (twins of 5) and Margaret (aged 4).

- *Do you think this family is typical?*
- *Can this picture tell us anything about the size of families in the sixteenth century?*
- *How does the artist suggest that the father is the head of the household?*

Bartlemewe Spiller was married to Alice Starr the xijth daie of April [1613].

Bartholomew Spyller the sonne of Thomas Spyller of Colyton was christened the xviijth day of August [1588].

Allis Starre the daughter of Anne Starre of Colyton beyng basse borne was christend the xvth daye of Novembre [1581].

Source E   *Part of a parish register.*

Source F

This is how one modern historian describes family size:

'Families were usually simple, containing parents and children. But richer households were bigger, containing living-in servants, and one in three households had at least one servant. People were not in service for life, but as youngsters before setting up their own homes.'

D. Palliser, *The Age of Elizabeth*, 1986

- Find out the average number of children in a family among the pupils in your class.

Source G

Some advice to young couples in the seventeenth century:

'When you get married, live by yourself with your wife in a family of your own.'

William Whately, *Vicar of Banbury*, seventeenth century.

Find evidence in this unit that proves or disproves the following theories.
- ◆ People got married when they were very young.
- ◆ People had large numbers of children.
- ◆ Young people lived with their parents after they got married.

Britain and the wider world

In 1500, European sailors were beginning to explore new lands overseas. In 1492, Christopher Columbus rediscovered the continent of America, the 'New World'. There were many more voyages of discovery in the next century, and new and valuable trade routes opened up.

Why did Britain join the voyages of exploration? What were the results?

Before 1500, people in Britain and Europe knew little about many parts of the world. Many may have believed travellers' fairy tales. They heard stories of frightening sea monsters, of fabulously rich lands, of strange plants and animals.

Over the next 200 years, improvements in ships and navigation made it possible for European sailors to travel further than ever before. They visited countries and crossed seas that many people had not known existed. Valuable gold and silver mines were discovered in America. Expensive silk cloth and new spices were brought back from the East, from India and China.

Source A

The first Europeans to be interested in voyages of exploration were the Spanish and Portuguese. Richard Hakluyt believed the British should copy them. Hakluyt was an English writer and clergyman. He wrote about the voyages that took place during his lifetime.

> 'The Kings of Spain and Portugal have enlarged their kingdoms, greatly enriched themselves and their subjects, and trebled the size of their navies. If we follow, there will be huge demands for English cloth, with what great benefit of all those who work in the cloth trade. A great number of men, but also children and women who now have no work, will be found employment in making things which can be traded with those who live in the new lands.'

Hakluyt had other ideas about why it was important for British sailors to explore the world.

> 'First, and most important, to spread the happy news of Jesus Christ to those who know nothing of Him. Second, to teach them about our knowledge of farming.'

For Hakluyt, like many others, the great prize was trade with the East. The East produced exotic spices, fine cottons and silks, and delicate porcelain, which were traded across slow, expensive routes overland. Hakluyt and many others believed that it must be possible to sail to China by charting a route around the north of Russia or the north of Canada. He encouraged sailors to look for new routes.

> 'See what islands and ports you might find by sailing to the north-east, for it would be good that we should have the control over our own trade routes to India and China, and so bring ourselves great riches.'

Richard Hakluyt, *The Principal Navigations, Voyages and Discoveries of the English Nation*, 1589–1600

Why did the British make voyages of exploration?

In fact, there was no route to the East by sailing north. But the voyages that searched for it were not useless. Martin Frobisher's attempt to sail around the north of Canada in 1576 helped to open up the Canadian fur and timber trade for Britain. And Hugh Willoughby and Richard Chancellor's attempt to sail around the north of Russia also brought new trading links for Britain.

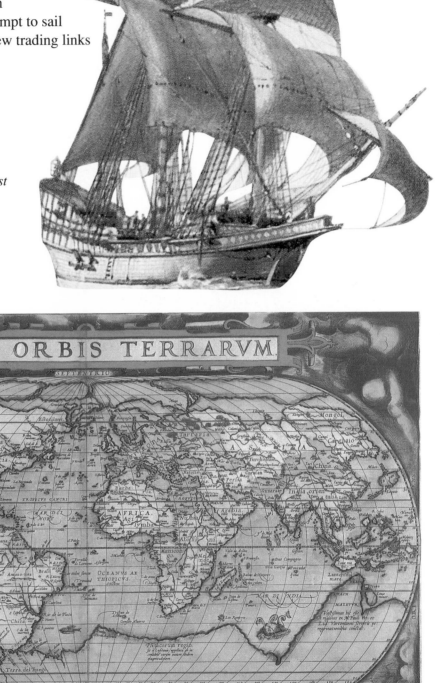

Source B *Between 1578 and 1580, Sir Francis Drake and his men became the first Englishmen to sail around the world. It was a raiding voyage. Drake brought back a huge treasure to Britain. This picture was painted 300 years later.*

Source C   *A map of the world, 1584. It was drawn by Abraham Ortelius.*

69

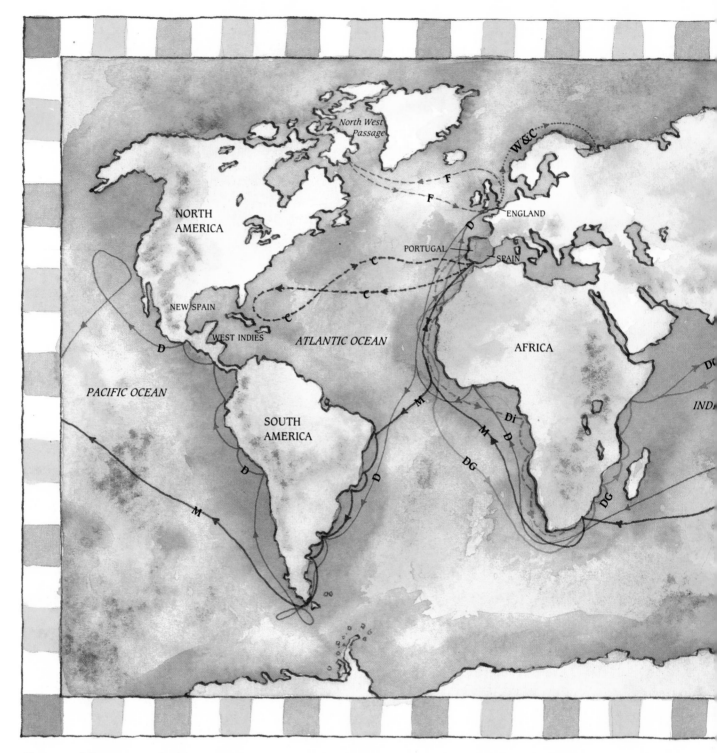

Voyages of discovery in the fifteenth and sixteenth centuries.

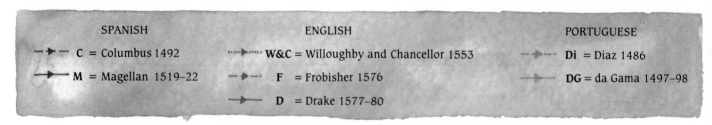

SPANISH	ENGLISH	PORTUGUESE
C = Columbus 1492	**W&C** = Willoughby and Chancellor 1553	**Di** = Diaz 1486
M = Magellan 1519–22	**F** = Frobisher 1576	**DG** = da Gama 1497–98
	D = Drake 1577–80	

From England, ships travelled to
- southern Europe, to trade in fruits
- the Baltic, to trade in fur and timber
- the East Indies, to trade in spices and new, light cloths
- the West Indies, to trade in sugar, tobacco and fruit
- North America, to trade in sugar and timber.

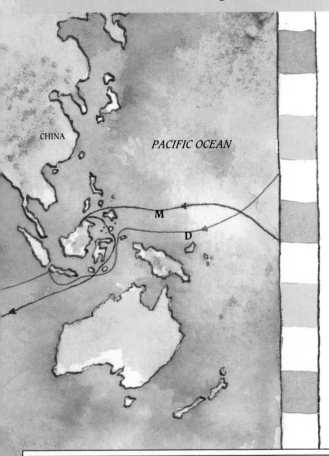

CHINA

PACIFIC OCEAN

M

D

1 Compare Source C with the map showing voyages of discovery. Which parts of the world did Ortelius seem to know most about? Which parts did he seem to know least about?

2 Why did British sailors set out on voyages of discovery? Use the evidence in this unit to fill in a table like the one below.

Reason for exploration	Source

Why do you think Richard Hakluyt's work is an important source for a historian?

The results of Britain's exploration and new trade

☆ War

More exploration led to more wars. In Queen Elizabeth I's reign, British seamen fought continually against the Spanish, capturing treasure as they did so. Later, Britain fought wars about trade against the Dutch and the French.

☆ Slavery

British traders became involved with the slave trade. British ships took Africans as slaves to America. There they worked on large plantations, producing sugar and cotton which was then shipped back to Britain. It was a very profitable business for the British, though at huge and terrible human cost.

☆ Wealth

Many people became very wealthy as a result of new trade routes. Bristol became one of the busiest and richest ports in the world.

☆ Settlement

Some people left Britain to settle, and often to control, the lands that had been explored. There were important new settlements in North America, where many Puritans set up new colonies, such as Virginia.

☆ New tastes and goods

Sugar from the West Indies, silks and cottons from the East, and spices from all over the world were brought back to Britain. New crops like potatoes and tobacco were first introduced to Britain from America in the sixteenth century. Tea and coffee had also been unknown in Britain before 1500.

☆ A powerful nation

The new trade made Britain very powerful. The East India Company, for example, which was founded in 1600, gradually increased its control over large parts of India. The British Crown controlled colonies in North America.

The Catholic Church

At the beginning of the sixteenth century, the Church in Western Europe was Catholic, as it had been in medieval times. The Church was very rich and powerful, and Church courts could punish people. The Church was led by the Pope in Rome. Most people in Britain were loyal members of the Church.

The Protestants

For centuries some people had criticised the Catholic Church for its extreme wealth and abuse of power. In Germany, a monk named Martin Luther started a fierce debate about the Church in 1517. Many people who were unhappy about the Catholic Church followed him. They set up a breakaway Church, and were called Protestants. By 1530 there were a small number of people in Britain who supported Luther's ideas.

Henry VIII and the Pope

Between 1530 and 1536 Henry VIII argued with the Pope. He wanted a divorce from his wife, Catherine of Aragon, but the Pope refused. So Henry rejected the Pope and made himself head of the Church in England, and Protestants supported him. This is called the 'Break from Rome'. The new 'Church of England' took up some important Protestant ideas. The power of the Pope in England came to an end.

Catholics versus Protestants

Changes in religion led to more than a hundred years of argument. Catholics were unhappy about the Church of England. Protestants thought that the changes had not gone far enough.

1500–1750

Magic and witches

Many ordinary people still believed in magic. Both Catholics and Protestants were unhappy about this. Until the end of the seventeenth century some women were accused of using magic, and were burnt as witches.

Plays for the people

There was great interest in the theatre. Before 1500 most plays were about religion. After 1500 plays were written about new themes. Playwrights like William Shakespeare and Christopher Marlowe wrote histories, tragedies and comedies. Famous plays like *Hamlet* are full of popular jokes as well as serious themes.

Art and architecture

Until 1500 much art and many buildings were produced for the Church. After 1500 this began to change. Artists throughout Europe became interested in other subjects such as Greek and Roman themes. In England, fine houses were built for rich merchants as well as noblemen. There were fires in many old wood-built towns and cities like London, which meant that these places had to be rebuilt.

Explaining the world

After 1500 people became more interested in trying to understand and explain the world around them. Improvements in technology meant that there were better scientific instruments. Some people such as Galileo in Italy began to study the stars, and others carried out investigations and experiments. This new science frightened many leaders of the Church. They thought it might challenge traditional beliefs about the world and the universe which came from the Bible.

22

What did people believe?

We know a lot about the way in which the Church was organised in the sixteenth and seventeenth centuries. But what did ordinary people actually believe?
How can we find out what they believed?

An international Church

All West European countries were part of the Roman Catholic Church. The Church was controlled by the Pope in Rome. The Pope appointed archbishops and bishops all over Europe. Church services and the Bible were all in Latin.

Pope

Cardinals

Archbishops

Bishops

Priests

Heaven and Hell

Everyone had to go to church. But it is difficult to find out what people actually believed in. This is because most people could not read or write, so we have very little evidence.

Paintings like Sources A and B give us some clues about people's beliefs. Everyone does seem to have believed in God, and in Heaven and Hell. They expected that God would appear and judge people, sending good people to Heaven and evil people to Hell. Many of them also believed that the world would end, perhaps in their lifetime.

How did these beliefs affect the way people behaved? Sources C, D and E give you some ideas about this. By using evidence like this very carefully, we can start to piece together people's ideas about religion.

Fifteenth-century images of Hell and the Garden of Eden, by the Dutch painter, Hieronymus Bosch.

Source A *Hell.*

Source B *The Garden of Eden.*

● *What effect would pictures like these have on the people who saw them?*

Source C

Keith Thomas is a modern historian. He tried to work out what ordinary poor people believed. This is how he describes some of their beliefs.

'Pregnant women were told by midwives to pray to St Margaret if they wanted to reduce the pain they felt in labour, or to call on St Felicitas if they wanted to be sure that their new child was a boy.'

Keith Thomas, *Religion and the Decline of Magic*, 1971

Source D

A piece from the body of a saint was known as a 'relic'. Relics were thought to have a special power that could help people with their prayers. In 1535 Henry VIII ordered his officers to carry out a survey of the monasteries. This is what they found at Bury St Edmunds.

'We found the coals that St Laurence was roasted with, the cuttings from St Edmund's fingernails, St Thomas of Canterbury's penknife and his boots, and a set of skulls which were said to cure headache. We found enough "pieces of the Holy Cross" to make a whole new cross out of, and other relics for all sorts of superstitions.'

John Ap Rice, 1535

Source E

Margaret Hoby was a rich woman who kept a diary. This is how she describes her day.

'In the morning after praying I wrote some notes on the Bible until ten o'clock. Then I went for a walk and when I came back I prayed and did some sewing. After dinner I walked again and did some things about the house until four. I wrote out a sermon preached the day before and read and prayed. After supper I prayed again and went to bed.'

Margaret Hoby, 1585

---

1 Which sources in this unit would you use to help you prove that:
◆ people in the sixteenth and seventeenth centuries thought religion was important
◆ people believed that the Devil was a real person
◆ people were superstitious
◆ people's beliefs were changing?

2 a Can you find any evidence in this unit that Bosch's ideas about Heaven and Hell (Sources A and B) were what ordinary people really did believe?

b There is no reason to suppose that prayers or relics actually worked. So why did people still use them?
c What superstitions do you have? Why do you continue to believe in them?

3 a Write down five things that people in the sixteenth and seventeenth centuries believed. Compare your list with your neighbour's. What differences are there?
b How does this help you to see why historians might disagree about what people in the sixteenth and seventeenth centuries believed?

23

The King's divorce

One of the most important changes to take place in England after 1500 was in religion. In 1500 England was a Catholic country, obedient to the Pope in Rome. By the middle of the century this had changed. There were huge arguments about religion for more than a hundred years.

What were the causes of this great change?

The state of the Church

The Catholic Church in England was wealthy and powerful. The Church and monasteries owned more than a third of all the land in England and many fine treasures. But many people, including some loyal churchmen, were unhappy about the Church.

John Longland was one of these people. In 1521 he became Bishop of Lincoln. He set out to find out how the Church was working in his area.

Source A   *This is a summary of what Longland found in Lincoln.*

● *How could we find out if Lincoln was typical of other areas?*

Problems for the King

In 1527 Henry VIII must have been very worried about his kingdom and the Church. The cartoon opposite shows us what his worries might have been. What could he do?

★ Most people seemed to be content with the Catholic Church. They gave generously for the repair of their churches. They often left money to the Church in their wills.

★ In some places, groups of people were listening to the new Protestant ideas from Germany. They wanted the Bible translated into English and an end to taxes being paid to Rome.

★ Over a quarter of vicars did not live in their parish. Many could not read or write and some could not say the Lord's Prayer.

★ A survey of the monasteries in the area showed that twelve were well-ordered, but nineteen of them had serious faults. These included:

– at Wellow the monks sat up at night drinking, kept hunting dogs and wandered into town whenever they wanted

– at Dorchester the prior kept a woman in his room, and monks raced greyhounds and played tennis.

I need a son. I have been married for nearly twenty years and my wife, Catherine of Aragon, has given me only a daughter. Who will inherit my throne when I die? Will the Pope let me divorce my wife?

The Church and its monasteries are very rich. I need money to pay for my luxurious court and my debts. If only I could get my hands on some of that wealth.

I spy an attractive new lady-in-waiting at court, Anne Boleyn. If only I could marry her instead.

My advisers tell me of the new Protestant ideas, which are spreading fast in Germany. Princes there are starting to throw out the Catholic Church.

The Church takes money from my country in taxes for Rome. It's used for grand buildings like St Peter's in Rome. What do we get in return?

Some people in England are welcoming the new Protestant ideas. They are saying that the Bible and church services should now be in English, not Latin.

---

1 Which of the following statements does Source A

a prove

b suggest but not *prove*

c disprove?

◆ 'The Catholic Church in England was in a dreadful state in the 1520s.'

◆ 'The biggest problems in the Church were to do with monasteries.'

◆ 'Ordinary people were fed up with the Catholic Church.'

◆ 'Some Church leaders wanted to improve the Church in the 1520s.'

◆ 'All monasteries were in a dreadful state: drinking and gambling were typical.'

2 Work in pairs. Study Source A, and draw up an action plan for John Longland which would help him to put right the problems in his area.

3 a Can you work out how these pairs of ideas were connected?

◆ Henry's unhappiness about his marriage *and* the Pope's powers

◆ Protests against the Church in Germany *and* the state of the Church in England

◆ Henry's money problems *and* the wealth of the monasteries

b Using the cartoon of Henry VIII, write a short passage to explain what Henry's biggest problems were in 1527.

4 The thought bubbles in the cartoon show what Henry might have been *thinking*. Write a speech bubble for him which sets out what he might have *done*.

24

The break with Rome

Between 1527 and 1535 Henry VIII and his ministers brought about great changes in the English Church.

What were these changes? What were their effects?

A Church of England

Source A

In the 1520s and 1530s Henry argued fiercely with the Pope in Rome. He persuaded Parliament to pass this new law.

> 'The King is the supreme Head of the Church of England. He has full power to change the Church.'

Act of Supremacy, 1534

After this law had been passed some important changes took place in the Church.

* Many Catholic beliefs were dropped.

* Henry closed down all the monasteries and nunneries in England.

* An English translation of the Bible appeared. Church services were in English instead of Latin.

* Henry's son Edward was taught by people who believed in Protestant ideas.

Source B *Fountains Abbey in North Yorkshire as it is today. This was one of the many monasteries closed down by Henry VIII in the 'Dissolution of the Monasteries' between 1536 and 1540.*

Henry VIII's changes in the Church took place against a complicated background. How can we understand these changes? In the list opposite, different things that affected religion in the sixteenth century have been muddled up. Some of them were *causes* of Henry's changes, and some were the *results*.

★ English Catholics who objected to Henry's changes were punished. Two leading Catholics, Thomas More and John Fisher, were executed in 1532.

In Yorkshire, thousands of people joined a protest in 1536 against the changes. Two hundred rebels were hanged. Some Catholics left England. They only returned when Henry's Catholic daughter, Mary, later became queen.

★ In Germany in 1517 a monk named Martin Luther argued with the Catholic Church. He broke away and set up a new Church. His followers were called Protestants.

★ Henry VIII wanted to divorce his first wife, Catherine of Aragon. Although Catherine and Henry had a daughter, Mary, they had no sons. Henry wanted a son to become the next king. In 1527 he fell in love with Anne Boleyn. He thought the Pope would let him divorce Catherine and marry Anne. The Pope refused because the Catholic Church did not usually allow divorce.

★ Late in 1533 Anne Boleyn became pregnant. It might be a son. Henry had to find a way of marrying her. He persuaded the Archbishop of Canterbury to ignore the Pope and give him a divorce. Then he married Anne.

★ Luther's Protestant ideas became popular with some people in Henry's court and some English churchmen. Henry's chief minister, Thomas Cromwell, was one of the most important.

Source C   *Between 1553 and 1558 Mary tried to restore Catholicism. More than 400 Protestants were burnt to death. After 1558, Catholic opponents of Elizabeth were executed.*

Why did people think that religion mattered so much? Perhaps one answer is given by Source D.

Source D

The author of this source became Elizabeth I's chief minister.

'No country can be safe where there is toleration of two religions. There is no hatred so great as that about religion. People who disagree about God will never agree how to serve their country.'

Sir William Cecil, 1581

● *For each set of events, try to work out whether they helped cause the break with Rome, or whether they were the results of the break.*

Protestants and Catholics

Henry VIII's changes did not end religious argument. They caused more. After Henry died, his son Edward pushed forward more Protestant changes. The next monarch, Queen Mary, then tried to bring back the Catholic Church. In 1558, Elizabeth I adopted a mostly Protestant Church.

Throughout the century, people who disagreed with the monarch about religion were often imprisoned or burnt to death. Later, more extreme Protestants thought that Elizabeth had not been Protestant enough. These people, called Puritans, pressed for even more changes in the Church.

1 Divide the list of religous changes into two lists: things that helped to cause the break with Rome, and things that were the result of the break. Add to each list any other causes or results of the break that you can think of.

2 How were the different things in each of your lists connected to each other?

3 a People in the sixteenth century were executed if they disagreed with the government about religion. How can you explain this? Use Source D to help you.
b Why are people not treated in this way in Britain today if they disagree with the government about religion?

25

Witchcraft

All over Europe between about 1520 and 1640, women were burnt or hanged as witches. In the 1640s the witch hunt was at its height in Britain.

Why was there a witch hunting craze?

A witch is hanged

In the sixteenth and seventeenth centuries, believing in the Devil and in spirits was as important as believing in Christ. Many people had a great fear of witches. A witch was someone who was believed to be possessed by the Devil.

In 1563 Parliament made a new law against witchcraft. The first trial for witchcraft in England took place in 1565. A woman called Agnes Waterhouse was accused of being a witch and hanged.

Why were people accused?

A small incident in a local community could have drastic results.

In 1582, 13 women from the village of St Osyth in Essex were tried for witchcraft. An old woman called Ursula Kemp was accused by her neighbours of being a witch. She said she was not guilty.

Source A

At the trial, one neighbour said:

'I'm poor and I could not pay Ursula Kemp. She asked for cheese as a payment but I had none to give her. She murmured that she would get even with me. Soon afterwards I was taken lame.'

A record of the St Osyth Witch Trial, 1582

● How would we explain an incident like this today?

Source B

Another neighbour gave this evidence.

'Ursula and I had a little matter of business between us, but I did not keep my side of the bargain, knowing Ursula to be a naughty beast. So Ursula, in revenge, bewitched my child. And as proof that it was Ursula who had so hurt the babe, the little creature of one year old, when I carried it past her house, cried, "Wo, wo," and pointed with its finger to the window.'

A record of the St Osyth Witch Trial, 1582

● What *evidence* is there that Ursula bewitched the child?

After a long trial, Ursula Kemp finally confessed that she was a witch and had put spells on people. She was hanged.

The Witch Finder General

In England witch hunting was at its height in the 1640s. A young man, Matthew Hopkins, claimed he had found thirty-six witches at work near Ipswich. They were arrested. Under torture most of them admitted that they were witches. Thirty-four were found guilty. Eighteen were executed. Hopkins called himself 'Witch Finder General'.

Matthew Hopkins Witch Finder Generall

My Imps names are

Holt

1 Ilemauzar
2 Pyewackett

Jarmara

3 Pecke in the Crowne
4 Griezzell Greedigutt

Sacke & Sugar

Newes

Vinegar Tom

Source C

The Witch Finder General. In this picture Matthew Hopkins is exposing two women as witches. The women are talking to their evil spirits, or 'familiars'.

● *What do you think the artist believed about witches?*

Source D

Arthur Wilson was at the trial of Hopkins' 'witches'. He did not believe they were guilty.

'I could see nothing in the evidence which persuaded me to think of them as anything but poor, envious, unhappy, underfed people whose imaginations would make them believe anything.'

Quoted in MacFarlane, *Witchcraft in Tudor and Stuart England*, 1970

Source E

John Gaule was a vicar in Huntingdonshire. In 1646 Matthew Hopkins wanted to visit the area to search for witches. Gaule did not want him to come, and he wrote a pamphlet explaining why.

'Every old woman with a wrinkled face, a furr'd brow, a hairy lip, a gobber tooth and a squint eye, a squeaking voice or a scolding tongue will be called a witch.'

Revd John Gaule, 1646

Why were there witch hunts?

Historians have asked two questions about the witch hunts: why did they start, and why did they come to an end soon after Matthew Hopkins tried the thirty-six Essex witches? The illustration here suggests some of the reasons historians have used to help explain why the witch craze started.

> Rising prices, enclosures and other changes made people stop trusting each other. They blamed other people for their problems.

> Everyone believed in Hell and the Devil. If things went wrong, people blamed the Devil.

> The Church was in trouble because of Protestantism. Protestant churches were suspicious of superstition and they punished superstitious people.

> Times were hard, especially during the Civil War. Because life was unsettled, people blamed witches for the problems.

1 What have the views expressed about the witches in Sources A and D got in common? What makes them different from each other?

2 Does the fact that people confessed to being witches *prove* that witchcraft was real in the sixteenth and seventeenth centuries?

3 Explain in your own words why you think the witch hunts happened.

26

Exploring the universe

Between 1500 and 1750 people became more and more interested in explaining the world around them. Attitudes to what we now call science, and nature, were changing.

Why was this?

Perhaps you have a science lesson today. Maybe you'll be doing an experiment. In the sixteenth century, no one would have used the words 'science' and 'experiment'. If people wanted to explain something mysterious, they often said that God, or the Devil, had caused it. By 1700 this attitude was changing. The important thinkers of the day were interested in medicine, mathematics, physics, astronomy, and many other subjects.

Before 1500, people in the West believed that the Earth was fixed at the centre of the universe. The Sun, the Moon and the other planets circled around the Earth. Their ideas were based on those of the great Greek philosopher, Aristotle, who lived about 2,300 years ago, in the fourth century BC. The Church supported the view that God created the Earth as the centre of the universe.

Look at the list of changes below. All these things were happening between 1500 and 1750. Each of them helps to explain why attitudes to science and nature were changing.

✷ After 1520 people began to challenge the Catholic Church, which had not been willing to think about new ideas about the world.

✷ Technological improvements between 1580 and 1620 meant that better instruments such as microscopes and telescopes were invented.

✷ In 1543 a Polish scholar called Copernicus wrote a book. In it he suggested that the Sun, not the Earth, was the centre of the universe. His ideas challenged those of the Church.

✷ In England during the Civil War, a group of educated men began to meet to discuss ideas. Charles II encouraged them and in 1662 named their organisation the Royal Society.

✷ In the 1620s an Italian named Galileo used a telescope to prove that Copernicus's ideas were correct. Galileo's works were banned by the Catholic Church.

✷ The printing press was introduced to Britain in the late fifteenth century. With printed books, ideas could spread more quickly across Europe.

✷ Francis Bacon, writing just after 1600, said that scientists should base their ideas on experiment and observation. Before this time, people had been used to developing ideas without testing them.

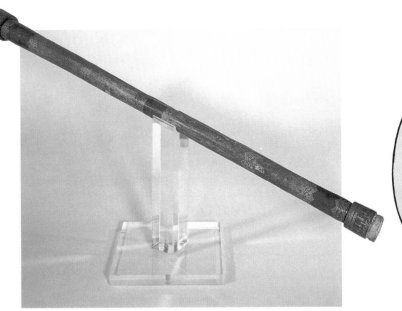

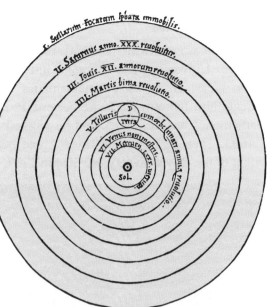

Source A *Telescopes like these, which had several lenses, were developed from about 1600. They made it possible for people to learn more about our universe.*

Source B *View of the universe, according to Copernicus's ideas.*

● *What is at the centre of the universe?*

PROSPECTUS INTRA CAMERAM STELLATAM.

Source C *The Royal Observatory was set up in Greenwich in 1673. It was designed by Christopher Wren for observing the skies.*

● *What does the picture tell you about the people's interest in the world about them?*

● *There are two portraits on the wall. Can you guess whose they might be?*

A scientist: Isaac Newton

Isaac Newton was born in 1642. At 18 he went to Cambridge University and became interested in scientific ideas. His work on mathematics and on light made him famous. At 26 he became Professor of Mathematics at Cambridge, and he worked there until 1693. Then he moved to London and became President of the Royal Society. He died in 1727.

According to a popular story, Newton's ideas about gravity were triggered when an apple fell on his head from a tree. This set him thinking about why some things, like an apple, fall to Earth, but other things, like the Moon, do not. In a book setting out his theories, Newton showed that planets are kept in place by two forces – their own speed, and the gravitational pull of the Sun upon them.

● The story about Newton and the apple is not true. Why do you think people still tell it?

Source D *A portrait of Sir Isaac Newton.*

What did Newton achieve?

★ Using mathematics, he showed that planets in the solar system are held together by a force he called 'gravity'.

★ He tried to explain the way the planets move round the Sun.

★ He found out that white light is a mixture of light of different colours.

★ He developed theories which explain the way objects move when force is applied to them.

1 Look at Source C. What evidence can you find in the picture about
◆ how people studied the skies
◆ how they recorded what they saw?

2 Look at the list of changes on page 82.
a Plan a diagram to show what helped to bring about changes in attitudes towards scientific subjects between 1500 and 1750.
b Which two causes do you think were the most important in bringing about these changes? Explain why you chose those two. Compare your answer with those of other people.

3 Find out if Newton's name is used in any of your science books. Can you suggest why a man who lived 300 years ago is still important to science today?

27

William Shakespeare: theatre for the people

William Shakespeare wrote more than thirty plays – comedies, tragedies and histories – between 1590 and 1612. They are still performed all over the world today.

Why is Shakespeare so important?

Travelling actors

What will you do when you get home from school tonight? Homework? Watch television? Now think again: there is no television. What entertainment will you look forward to? How will you hear the news?

There was no television or radio in the sixteenth century. Entertainment – and news – came from bands of travelling actors, who moved on foot around the country, hoping to attract audiences. Young and old gathered to see these actors perform. The scripts of their plays varied at each performance, and there was plenty of scope for including jokes about recent news, the latest fashions, or the King and Queen.

Also popular were the religious plays, or 'mystery plays'. They were based on Bible stories, and were performed inside or outside churches and cathedrals. They were widely performed in medieval times, but were still popular in the sixteenth century.

The first English theatres

After about 1550, these entertainments began to change. Actors still travelled, but instead of performing on temporary stages in the market-place, inn-yard, church or street, the idea of plays in a purpose-built theatre began to develop. What were the early theatres like?

Source A

This is a modern account of early theatres.

'The theatre was a wooden building forming a circular enclosure around an open courtyard. In this courtyard stood the stage. Around the yard were three galleries, one above the other, with seats for the spectators. In the yard the audience had to stand. There was no roof.'

C. Walter Hodges, *Shakespeare's Theatre*, 1965

A modern artist's impression of the Globe Theatre in London, where Shakespeare worked, wrote and acted his plays. It was one of the first theatres, built in 1598. The white flag was hoisted when the weather was fine, to show that a performance was going to take place.

● What was the advantage of having a fixed place for a theatre?

Source B *William Shakespeare was born in 1564 in Stratford-upon-Avon in Warwickshire. There he went to the local grammar school. At 18 he married Anne Hathaway, and a few years later he went to London to become an actor with a company. He probably began to write plays in the late 1580s.*

86

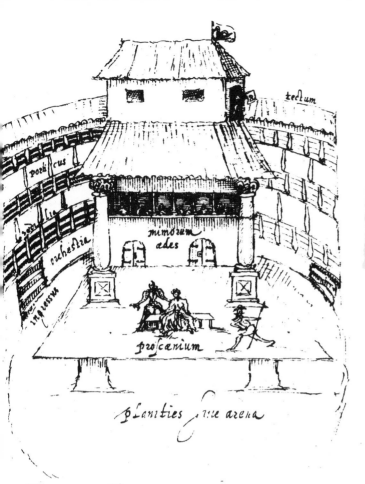

Source C
This sixteenth-century drawing shows the inside of the Swan Theatre, also in London, which was built in 1595.

● *How does the design of this theatre compare with the theatres of Ancient Rome?*

Shakespeare's audiences

Today, many people still enjoy watching performances of Shakespeare's plays. Nowadays, though, the theatre is expensive and not everyone can afford to go – or wants to. But Shakespeare's plays were written for *everyone*. In his day they were very popular with all kinds of people, rich and poor, young and old. And going to the theatre was not just a matter of going to see a play. There would be food, drink and side-shows in the open air.

Source D

'Look at the plays in London and the crowds of people who flock to see them!'

From a sermon preached in St Paul's Cathedral in 1577

Source E

This was written by a German visitor to London in 1599.

'Those who stand while they watch pay a penny. Those who want to sit pay another penny, and the most comfortable seats, which have cushions and a good view, cost three pennies. There is food and drink carried around the audience during the play.'

Thomas Platter, *Travels in England*, 1599

● What are the most popular forms of entertainment today? Which draw the largest crowds?

Shakespeare's language

Shakespeare is important for another reason too: his plays use all sorts of different types of language. He used the language of everyday life, and the language of the rich at court. He used ideas from English folk tales, and ideas from other countries. His plays contain a range of different types of characters, from kings to grave-diggers, who speak a vast range of language.

Although some of the language may sound strange to us today, many of the phrases that Shakespeare used are part of our everyday speech. It was Shakespeare who wrote down phrases like 'to the manner born', 'it's all Greek to me', it has 'seen better days', 'blinking idiot', and many others. How much of our everyday speech is still affected by Shakespeare? These phrases are commonly used today, and were used by Shakespeare.

I slept not one wink last night.

Don't stand on ceremony - come in!

It's all Greek to me...

I insist on *fair play*.

She's a real tower of strength.

That old thing's seen better days!

● Can you add any more to the list?

Shakespeare's England

There is, perhaps, one more reason why Shakespeare is so important. In 1588 England was in danger from a foreign enemy. A great fleet of about 130 ships set out from Catholic Spain to invade Protestant England. The Spanish Armada was defeated in the English Channel and almost completely destroyed by bad weather. England was saved from invasion, and Queen Elizabeth I became even more popular.

Shakespeare wrote most of his plays after 1590, soon after Spain had been defeated. His plays often express the pride which many people might have felt about England at that time. His history plays try to tell the history of England over the previous 200 years. Often, the history he writes is inaccurate, or simply made up. But he was not trying to write accurate history. Instead, he was trying to show how the Tudors and some of their ancestors made England peaceful and strong.

● What words does Shakespeare use to describe England? What impression of England does he create?

	Similar to modern theatre	Different from modern theatre
How theatres were built Types of play Audiences		

1 How were Tudor theatres similar to and different from modern theatres? Use the evidence in this unit to draw up and complete a table like the one above.

2 No Tudor theatres have survived. The top picture on page 86 is a modern attempt to work out what the Globe Theatre looked like.
◆ Where do you think the artist's information came from?
◆ How could we start to find out whether or not the picture is reliable?

3 Which of the following ideas can you prove by using the evidence in this unit?
◆ The theatre was very popular in the sixteenth century.
◆ Rich *and* poor people went to the theatre.
◆ Plays were performed in the open air.
◆ Elizabeth I went to see Shakespeare's plays.
In each case, say which pieces of evidence, if any, prove the point.

4 a What different reasons can you find in this unit to help explain why Shakespeare was so important in the history of the theatre?
b Why do historians as well as dramatists find it useful to study Shakespeare's plays?

Wren: rebuilding London

London, 2 September 1666: disaster struck when the Great Fire of London swept across the city. It started in a baker's shop, and soon burnt down most of the city of London, where many houses were built of wood.

How important was Christopher Wren in rebuilding London?

Source A *The Great Fire of London, 1666. It began in Pudding Lane, close to the river, and burnt for a week. This picture was painted by an eye-witness to the Fire.*

The fire swept through the city, burning down the wooden houses that nestled close together in the narrow streets. More than 13,000 houses were destroyed. Churches, halls and public buildings were also burnt down, and gone too was London's great cathedral, St Paul's. Amazingly, only twenty people died.

Soon after the fire, plans for rebuilding the city began to be drawn up. The King and his Council turned to Christopher Wren.

89

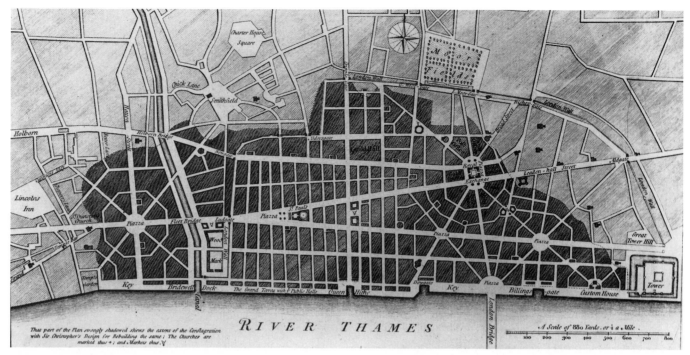

Source B *Wren's suggested plan for rebuilding London after the Great Fire. It was never carried out: Londoners preferred to rebuild the old maze of narrow streets. The darkly shaded area on the plan shows the area damaged by fire.*

● *Wren was partly inspired by Rome. How many new 'piazzas' (Italian for 'place' or 'square') can you see?*

Source C *Sir Christopher Wren (1632–1723). The cathedral of St Paul's has been included in this portrait of the great architect and designer.*

Source D *The new St Paul's Cathedral, designed by Wren after the Fire. Wren's design was unique in Britain. He took ideas from Ancient Greece and Rome. His design included a central dome, pinnacles and decorated columns. It was officially completed in 1711.*

90

A PROSPECT of the CITY of LONDON.

Source E *A view of London in 1710. Wren designed fifty-three new churches. Twenty-five of them still stand today, although their spires and towers are often hidden by modern buildings.*

● *How many churches can you count in this picture?*

Who was Christopher Wren?

Unlike today, there was no special training for architects. Christopher Wren was trained in mathematics and astronomy. He believed that buildings should be based on mathematical ideas: they should be symmetrical, and based on mathematical principles. He had travelled widely and took ideas from Italy and France and from Ancient Greece and Rome.

Wren saw the rebuilding of London as a chance to redesign the whole city. It was a great opportunity to widen the streets and improve the houses. Only nine days after the fire Christopher Wren gave Charles II his plan for a new London: it included broad avenues and open squares instead of the narrow alleys of the old city.

In fact, many of Wren's plans were never used. People said they were too expensive and that rebuilding had to start immediately. But fifty-three new churches and the new St Paul's Cathedral were built in London to Wren's design. By the time he died in 1723, he had shaped a new city.

---

1 What information about the Fire of London is it possible to get from Source A?

2 What sources in this unit would you use to prove that
◆ Wren was influenced by the ideas he took from mathematics
◆ Wren was influenced by buildings of Ancient Greece and Rome
◆ Wren was unable to carry out his most ambitious plans for London?

3 Look again at Source A, and at Source E. Make a list of the ways in which London was the same before and after the fire, and the ways in which it was different.

4 'By the time he died in 1723, Wren had shaped a new city.' Does the evidence in this unit support or disprove this statement?

A changing Britain?

You have now looked at Britain between 1500 and 1750.

What does it have to do with us today? Why should we study Britain's past?

Do the changes that took place between 1500 and 1750 still affect us now? If we look at people in the past, can we understand more about ourselves?

Look at the pictures on pages 92 and 93 before you try to answer these questions about then and now.

● What are the similarities?

Source A
Queen Elizabeth II reading the 'Queen's Speech' at the State Opening of Parliament today.

Source B
The Speaker of the House of Commons being presented to Queen Elizabeth I in 1603.

Source C
Rush hour on the new London Bridge in 1990.

Source D
The old London Bridge in 1620.

Source E
A timeless scene? The English countryside around Dixton Manor, Gloucestershire in the 1730s and (inset) the same scene today.

Attainment target grid

This grid is designed to indicate the varying emphases on attainment targets in the questions in each unit. It is not to be interpreted as a rigid framework, but as a simple device to help the teacher plan the study unit.

✗   some focus
✗✗   strong focus
✗✗✗   main focus

	AT 1			AT 2	AT 3
	a	b	c		
Introduction: Britain in 1500				✗✗	✗✗✗
1 A divided Britain?					✗✗✗
2 What problems did the Tudors and Stuarts face?		✗✗			✗✗✗
3 The rise of Parliament		✗✗✗			
4 James I and the Divine Right of Kings		✗✗			✗✗✗
5 Charles I: ruling without Parliament				✗	✗✗✗
6 Civil war!	✗✗	✗✗✗			
7 Taking sides		✗✗		✗✗✗	✗
8 Why did Parliament win?		✗✗✗	✗✗		
9 Weapons and tactics: Naseby 1645		✗✗			✗✗✗
10 The King is executed			✗✗✗	✗✗	✗✗
11 Oliver Cromwell: dictator?			✗	✗✗	✗✗✗
12 Cromwell in Ireland		✗✗		✗✗✗	
13 Charles II and the Restoration			✗✗✗		✗
14 1688: year of revolution			✗✗	✗✗✗	✗✗
15 Britain – a United Kingdom?			✗✗	✗✗✗	
16 Change in the countryside		✗✗✗	✗✗		✗
17 Change in the towns: London	✗✗		✗		✗✗✗
18 The lives of the poor					✗✗✗
19 The lives of women					✗✗✗
20 The family				✗✗✗	
21 Britain and the wider world		✗✗✗			✗✗
22 What did people believe?			✗✗✗	✗✗	✗✗
23 The King's divorce			✗✗✗		✗
24 The break with Rome		✗✗✗	✗✗		
25 Witchcraft		✗✗✗		✗✗	✗
26 Exploring the universe	✗✗	✗✗✗			✗
27 William Shakespeare: theatre for the people	✗		✗✗✗	✗✗	✗
28 Wren: rebuilding London			✗✗✗		✗✗

Index